DEALING WITH DRINK

Ian Davies and Duncan Raistrick

British Broadcasting Corporation

Ian W Davies
is Director of the Leeds Council on Alcoholism

Duncan S Raistrick
is Consultant in Charge, Addiction Unit, Leeds

This book is published in conjunction with the BBC
Continuing Education Radio series *Dealing with Drink*
first broadcast in Study on 4 on Monday evenings
11.00-11.30 pm, starting on 28 September 1981

The series is produced by Christopher Stone

Typesetting in 9/10½ point Palatino Linotron 202
by Input Typesetting Limited, London
Printed in England by Spottiswood Ballantyne Limited
Colchester, Essex

© The Authors 1981
First Published 1981
Published by the British Broadcasting Corporation
35, Marylebone High Street, London W1M 4AA
ISBN 0 563 16489 1

Contents

List of figures

Foreword by Sir George Young
Formerly Parliamentary Under Secretary of State for Health and Personal Social Services.

People have drunk alcohol throughout history. Drinking is for most people a pleasure which enlivens social occasions and helps relaxation. Unfortunately, some people are not always able to drink sensibly, and for them alcohol can cause major problems.

In recent years, we have seen in this country and abroad a significant growth in the number of deaths attributed to alcohol and in the number of men and women admitted to hospitals for the treatment of disorders and chronic illnesses which are alcohol-related. These trends have been matched by growth in other indicators of alcohol misuse such as convictions for drunkenness, and for drinking and driving offences, and the number of road traffic accidents where alcohol has been a factor.

This growth in alcohol misuse must be a cause of concern for everyone. The more alcohol is misused with harmful effects, the greater is the burden which all of us have to carry – in terms of scarce health and social services diverted from other priorities, diminished industrial performance and the overall tax burden that care of the casualties of misuse entails; and many families are tragically affected.

The harm caused by alcohol misuse can be much reduced if people learn to drink sensibly and if problem drinkers are helped at a very early stage. The many members of the caring professions have an essential role to play in the general alerting of people to the adverse effects of alcohol and in identifying, assessing and responding to problem drinking.

Sadly, many members of these professions are not aware that the misuse of alcohol may underlie many of the difficulties which they encounter in their day to day dealings with clients or patients and that responding to the drinking, although apparently a discouraging task, may in the long run be more effective and less time consuming than patching up the consequences. Social workers, health visitors, general practitioners, probation officers, teachers and others often lack confidence in their own ability to deal with problem drinking which they see as a 'special' condition always requiring the intervention of 'special' services.

The special services do have a role, but this handbook and the BBC series which it complements have the important aim of persuading members of all the caring professions that they also have an important role, and that for this role they can draw on skills which they already possess. The handbook provides them with useful background information and practical advice on what could otherwise be a daunting challenge. It should also be helpful to the employers, colleagues, friends and families of problem drinkers. I hope that it leads to greater awareness, greater confidence and greater effectiveness in our response to this serious problem.

Introduction

This handbook is for you

Thousands of people do not realise they are dealing with problem drinkers in their day to day work. This book is for them:

GPs	Nurses	Health visitors
Hospital doctors	Counsellors	Social workers
Midwives	Probation officers	Prison staff
District nurses	Police officers	Welfare staff
Teachers	Lecturers	Clergymen
Student health staff	Personnel officers	Youth workers
Citizens' advice bureaux' staff	Marriage guidance counsellors	Occupational health staff
Samaritans	Housing aid workers	

. . . and the list could go on. This handbook is also intended for anyone who wants to help a relative, friend or work colleague with a drink problem.

The approach

There is no shortage of academic works on the subject of alcoholism but until now there have been very few attempts to put a practical, working handbook into print. This handbook is based on our own experiences and we have combined these with what we see as the most useful current thinking on alcoholism. We hope that the result is a set of clear, easy-to-refer-to guidelines.

The aim

There can be no substitute for personal experience but we hope that this handbook will be of use to anyone who wants to help a problem drinker. There are three stages to helping. The first is *detection*, when someone is positively identified as

9

a problem drinker. The second is *assessment,* when the problem drinker is encouraged to talk about his drinking and his problems. This is also the time when the helper can try to decide how serious the problem is and what is the most appropriate *intervention* – the third stage. It is possible for one person to be involved at all three stages but a specialist alcohol agency may be called in at any time.

We also hope that the handbook will be useful when it comes to *alcohol education* for both professional groups and for the community, especially young people. Our hope is that better education will help the *prevention* of problem drinking in the future.

How to use the handbook
The best way to use the handbook is to read it through from cover to cover first of all. This should give you an idea of how widespread alcohol related problems are and of the roles played by the various people and agencies involved in helping the 'alcoholic'. After this you should make a note of the chapters which apply particularly to you and reread them.

The handbook has been extensively cross-referenced and in each chapter there are Checklists which summarise the main points. These should help you to refer quickly to any section. The chapters of the book can be grouped together as follows:

Chapter 1 looks at how ideas about alcoholism have changed in recent years.

Chapters 2, 3, 4, 5 and 6 deal mainly with the *detection* of the problem drinker.

Chapter 7 covers *assessment.*

Chapters 8, 9, 10 and 11 examine the options for *intervention.*

Chapter 12 looks at *alcohol education* for young people and at how you can identify 'at risk' children.

Chapter 13 has some ideas for 'do-it-yourself' alcohol education.

Chapter 14 discusses some of the awkward situations you might get into dealing with problem drinkers.

'Alcoholics' and problem drinkers

In this handbook, the terms are synonymous. The 'alcoholic' or problem drinker is someone whose life has been affected in terms of physical, psychological or social wellbeing by his dependence on alcohol. He may be anything from mildly to severely dependent.

'Alcoholic' does *not* refer solely to the single, homeless problem drinker. Alcoholism is used as a convenient shorthand to refer to all the problems connected with alcohol dependence.

Women and alcohol

The greatest increase in problem drinking is among women. It is not yet known exactly why this should be but it seems that it may have something to do with the availability of alcohol in more and more shops and with the increased social acceptability of women drinking. A collection of articles on *Women and Alcohol* was published in 1980 (see Appendix 3) which examined some of the particular problems faced by women 'alcoholics'.

In this handbook, wherever 'he' is mentioned it must, in most cases, be taken to include 'she' as well.

Note: In some sections of the handbook, notably those which deal with facilities for treatment and with the law as it relates to alcohol, references may apply only to England and Wales. You should check with local information sources.

Ian Davies
Duncan Raistrick

1 Alcoholism – a changing view

Introduction

Most of us in Great Britain enjoy having a drink. Social drinking is an established part of our way of life and it is true to say that alcohol will never cause the vast majority of us any long lasting problems. We need to remember, however, that alcohol can be dangerous and that it is the country's most abused drug. Current research suggests that some 750,000 people have a drink problem or could, using the term loosely, be called 'alcoholics'.

Until relatively recently the 'alcoholic' was seen as a figure of fun, someone to jibe at who was weak-willed, anti-social and who really ought to be able to demonstrate more self-control. Popular myth had it that 'alcoholics' were male, rough, dirty, lived on the streets and slept wherever they could. The truth is that only 5% of 'alcoholics' fit into this category. The rest are distributed throughout the community of which we are all part.

Attitudes to 'alcoholics' and alcoholism began to change slowly with the development of Alcoholics Anonymous (AA) which was founded in the USA in 1935 and with the work of the American alcohol specialist E M Jellinek.

The growth of self-help and AA

The services offered by AA are discussed in detail in Chapter 8 but, historically, AA arose in the climate of increased concern for human welfare which followed the depression as one of a number of self-help movements. It was (and still is) a lay organisation. At that time professional workers were not really involved in the care of the 'alcoholic'. AA pioneered the humanistic idea that the 'alcoholic' is someone who is ill and needs to be treated with the same care and concern given to anyone suffering from a chronic illness. The outlook for the 'alcoholic' became very much brighter and he was viewed more sympathetically by the general public. AA saw alcoholism as an allergy to alcohol.

The work of E. M. Jellinek

In the late fifties Jellinek's work was interpreted as supporting the concept of alcoholism as a disease. Even then, however, people did not appreciate the extent of the problem. For example, when Jellinek visited Britain he was told, apparently by an adviser to the Ministry of Health, that alcoholism was not a problem here and that he was wasting his time. Despite attitudes such as this, his work has subsequently had an enormous influence on the thinking of both the layman and the specialist.

Jellinek speculated that there were five species of alcoholism and he named each one after a letter of the Greek alphabet:

Alpha	A psychological dependence on alcohol
Beta	Heavy drinking resulting in physical damage
Gamma	Physical dependence accompanied by loss of control
Delta	Complete inability to abstain from alcohol even for short periods of time
Epsilon	Episodic heavy drinking

Jellinek felt that the *Gamma* and *Delta* species were by far the most common, and these were the ones he saw as the disease varieties. He suggested that once an 'alcoholic' began drinking he would lose control and find himself unable to stop. In other words, because an 'alcoholic' was suffering from an illness, his drinking was not really under conscious control.

Although similar to the position of Alcoholics Anonymous, Jellinek's was slightly different in some important respects. Unlike AA he suggested that an 'alcoholic' did not lose control over his drinking every time he took alcohol. He also felt that heavy drinking was initially a result of learning and that the disease of alcoholism developed at some point as drinking became increasingly excessive. Some AA members, on the other hand, implied that people could have alcoholism despite the fact they had always been teetotal. Further, they regarded 'alcoholics' who had been abstinent for many years as still having the disease of alcoholism albeit in a masked state.

Whilst Jellinek actually specified only five species of the illness of alcoholism he argued that there could well be many more. Essentially, he envisaged a progressive line or continuum of alcoholism ranging from mildly 'alcoholic' to severely 'alcoholic' although he did place more emphasis on the severely 'alcoholic' (*Gamma* and *Delta*) varieties. This idea of a continuum was to become popular among alcohol specialists over a decade later.

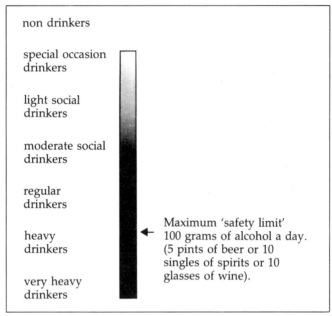

Figure 1: The continuum of alcohol dependence

Alcoholism as a disease

Despite the differences in their theories, there is little doubt that Alcoholics Anonymous and E. M. Jellinek were influential in establishing the popular view of alcoholism as a disease. This view of alcoholism is often known as the disease model and it produces some predictions and assumptions about the nature of alcoholism and the 'alcoholic'. Some of them have become part of the accepted wisdom without really receiving much scientific scrutiny:

- *It is more than just the amount of alcohol an 'alcoholic' consumes which makes him an 'alcoholic'*

  If alcoholism is seen as a disease then, by definition, 'alcoholics' have the disease. This implies that 'alcoholics' are, in a sense, qualitatively different from 'non-alcoholics'. This has been interpreted as suggesting that even someone who has not touched a drop for many years or even decades still suffers from the disease. AA calls this group 'recovering alcoholics'.

- *Alcoholism has a biological and genetic basis*

  Leading on from the first point, the disease model has been interpreted as meaning that alcoholism has a definite physical basis – a biochemical lesion in the brain. Some members of AA believe that there are people who have an as yet undiscovered but specific biological predisposition to alcoholism, though many scientists and clinicians would argue that you can still see alcoholism as a disease without necessarily having its cause as the focus. It follows that if people believe that alcoholism is a biological disorder then it is mainly a result of genetic rather than environmental factors.

- *Loss of control*

  Perhaps the most far reaching assumption made by those who see alcoholism as an illness concerns the idea of 'loss of control', an irresistible urge or craving for alcohol once a small amount has been drunk. This is taken to mean that the inevitable consequence of one or two drinks is continued drinking to the point of complete intoxication. Alcoholics Anonymous emphasises this and strongly encourages its members to remain totally abstinent. AA feels that people with the predisposition can never safely use alcohol in any form at all. The 'loss of control' idea really means that for the 'alcoholic' a choice as to whether he may drink again or not is no longer possible.

- *Once an 'alcoholic' always an 'alcoholic'*

  If alcoholism is regarded as a disease or allergy then unless this is cured directly by a particular type of drug or even an operation the illness remains. As no such treatments have been discovered, the disease model of alcoholism predicts that, once a person has been diagnosed as having the illness, he will never be able to change from the drinking pattern associated with alcoholism to the drinking pattern associated with normal drinking. In other words an 'alcoholic' will always remain a potential 'alcoholic'.

The disease model of alcoholism questioned

For many years the predictions and assumptions advanced by the advocates of the disease model (and outlined above) were the accepted principles of alcoholism treatment but they were not really based on practical experience. In the sixties, however, the situation seemed to change and people became more aware of the need to assess some of the traditional assumptions more rigorously.

- **Once an 'alcoholic'**
  Two lines of research marked a distinct change in the scientific, if not the popular, thinking on alcoholism. The first was a survey in 1962 which cast some doubt on the assumption that 'alcoholics' could not return to normal drinking. A long-term follow-up assessment of 'alcoholics' who had been treated in hospital many years previously and then discharged revealed that a small group of these people had been drinking normally for most of the time since leaving hospital. These findings cast some doubt on the assumption that an 'alcoholic' always remained an 'alcoholic'. Since then other surveys have produced roughly similar results.

- **Loss of control**
  The second major line of research in the mid-sixties involved giving alcohol to 'alcoholic' patients in a clinical setting and monitoring what happened. The prototype study was carried out by a psychiatrist called J. Merry. 'Alcoholics' were given small amounts of alcohol either surreptitiously or with their full knowledge. He found that if a patient was unaware that he had just drunk alcohol there was little evidence of increased craving or loss of control. The patients who were aware that they had been given alcohol reported some slight craving. Similar studies have been carried out since and have demonstrated clearly that alcohol given to 'alcoholics' in a clinical setting does not lead to the 'loss of control' predicted by the popular idea of the disease model.

- **There is something about an 'alcoholic's' make-up which makes him an 'alcoholic'**

  A rather less dramatic but equally important line of research has been the analysis of alcohol consumption in the general population. Essentially, the results of this research indicate that the distribution of alcohol consumption is roughly similar to that of any other pleasurable behaviour in which people can over-indulge such as gambling, sex, eating, smoking and television viewing. The distribution is what statisticians describe as unimodal. This means that the 'alcoholic' population is *not* a separate group as distinct from the normal population.

  On the contrary, it indicates that both normal drinkers and abnormal drinkers are part of the continuum on which the 'alcoholic' population is defined by an arbitrary cut off point (see page 16). Although data like this on alcohol consumption is notoriously difficult to obtain, there does seem to be some indication that 'alcoholics' are perhaps different from the rest of us only because of the amount they drink.

- **Genetics**

  Genetic studies of 'alcoholics' have produced no definitive evidence of any link and, as yet, no specific biological factors have been shown to precede all alcohol abuse.

  These are some of the lines of evidence which have led some clinicians and scientists to question the disease model of alcoholism. Others have been proposed in its place. Alcoholism can be seen as something which is culturally learned (social model), as a result of childhood experiences (analytic model) or as a lack of willpower (moral model). However, perhaps the most influential in recent years has been the behavioural model.

The behavioural model of alcoholism

The advocates of a behavioural approach regard excessive drinking as nothing more than too many movements of the right elbow, each of which transports an alcoholic liquid to the mouth: a behaviour. Whilst they acknowledge that the drug alcohol does have specific effects, they see drinking in the same light as they see other behaviours which we learn such as eating and smoking. They say that excessive drinking is a similar behaviour to overeating and heavy smoking. Behaviourists see a clear relationship between how often and how much a person indulges in any behaviour and its consequences. If a person eats too much he will become obese, if a person smokes too often and too much he may suffer from bronchitis or lung cancer. In both cases there may be all sorts of emotional, financial and social problems; it may be difficult to find clothes which fit if you are overweight and a hacking cough is not particularly attractive to other people.

When it comes to excessive drinking, the primary interest is in looking at the patient and assessing in detail why he is drinking too much. It may be because of his work, because of tension or a variety of other reasons. The answer is rarely simple. After this, some thought is given to ways in which his environment (emotional and social as well as physical) may be reorganised to encourage him to change his drinking habits. This form of treatment is outlined in detail in Chapter 9.

Critics complain that the behavioural model is too simplistic and cannot readily explain the repeated and apparently illogical episodes of the sheer self-destructive behaviour of many problem drinkers or 'alcoholics'.

Which model is correct?

Is the disease model correct and the behavioural model wrong? (That is, is alcoholism a special weakness and susceptibility to the drug alcohol rather than a behaviour which can be modified?) Or the other way round? The answer is that neither is wrong. Better than to ask 'which is correct?' is to ask 'given the present state of knowledge of alcoholism, which model gives the best account of the situation?', 'which model suggests the best ways of dealing with alcoholism?' and 'which model fits in best with reality?'

Undoubtedly, in the fifties and sixties the disease model fitted in with what was known and produced a treatment approach which has helped many people and will continue to do so. Today, however, with cracks appearing in the disease model, many people feel that the behavioural model reflects recent scientific advances better, though future discoveries may mean that the disease model becomes relevant again.

Alcohol Dependence Syndrome

One thing which all the ideas and theories we have looked at so far have in common is that they try to show how alcoholism is caused. On the other hand, Alcohol Dependence Syndrome, a recent innovation in alcohol studies, does not try to imply a cause but rather pieces together symptoms which, taken as a whole, indicate that a person has a drink problem. Because Alcohol Dependence Syndrome does not try to ascribe a cause to the problem, it can be used in conjunction with any of the 'models' described earlier.

In fact, because alcoholism and 'alcoholic' (though still useful shorthand references) have become so closely associated with the disease model, Alcohol Dependence Syndrome has replaced the word alcoholism in the International Classification of Diseases. Alcohol Dependence Syndrome is defined as, 'A state, psychic and usually also physical, resulting from taking alcohol, characterised by behavioural and other responses that include compulsion to take alcohol on a continuous or periodic basis in order to experience psychic effects, sometimes to avoid the discomfort of its absence; tolerance may or may not be present.'

We move on now to outline some of the symptoms or markers which make up Alcohol Dependence Syndrome and which indicate that someone may have a drink problem. They are not given any formal weighting or listed in order of priority and not all of them have to be present for someone to have a drink problem. Equally, it does not necessarily mean that someone is a problem drinker because he shows some of the symptoms of alcohol dependence. Each case you come across is individual and these makers are no more than guidelines.

● ***Alcohol Dependence Syndrome Markers***

Withdrawal symptoms
The common withdrawal symptoms include nausea, irritability, the 'shakes' and sweats. Severe withdrawal symptoms such as delirium tremens (DTs) or fits are less useful as markers because they are relatively uncommon (see Chapter 2).

Tolerance to alcohol
Generally, it can be said that the more a person drinks the more he needs to drink in order to achieve a given height of effect. In other words, he becomes more tolerant to alcohol (see Chapter 2). Having said this, it should be added that personality and the situation in which drink is taken can also have an effect. Increased tolerance to alcohol can often indicate increased dependence.

Variation in drinking habits
As a person moves along the dependency continuum (see Figure 1 on page 16) his drinking habits often begin to vary less and less. He tends to stick to the same drink in the same amounts at roughly the same time every day.

Importance of drinking behaviour
This is an attempt to assess how much importance someone places on drinking at the expense of other important aspects of his life such as family responsibilities and work. The circles in Figure 2 represent the changing importance given to family, work and alcohol, and can indicate stages in the drift towards greater dependency.

Relief drinking
As a person becomes more severely dependent on alcohol he can be increasingly aware that he drinks specifically to avoid withdrawal symptoms.

Thinking about alcohol
A person may begin to think about drink and drinking almost all the time, even against his conscious wishes. He may also experience a compulsion to drink, especially after the first few drinks of a session. This is similar to the original loss of control notion (see page 17) but is expressed more in terms of thoughts and attitudes. It does not have the fatalistic flavour of inevitability of the original idea.

Return to the original drinking pattern after abstinence
The speed with which a person returns to his original drinking pattern after a period of abstinence if some alcohol is taken also seems to be related to how dependent he is on alcohol.

It has often been emphasised by the advocates of Alcohol Dependence Syndrome that these ideas are provisional and that these notions are only guidelines.

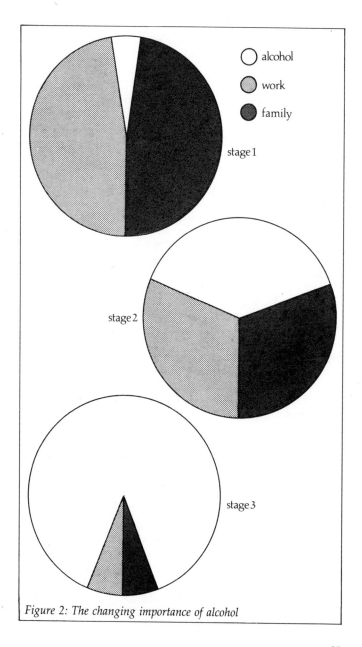

○ alcohol
● work
● family

stage 1

stage 2

stage 3

Figure 2: The changing importance of alcohol

In practice, it is complicated and demanding to get full information on every aspect of a person's drinking and different helpers will place greater emphasis on different aspects. Nonetheless there do seem to be some warning signs that someone may have a drink problem. The presence or the extent of withdrawal symptoms seems to be particularly important, especially if someone drinks in order to relieve these symptoms. Some would say that increased tolerance is also an important indicator of dependence on alcohol.

The implications of Alcohol Dependence Syndrome

The implications of Alcohol Dependence Syndrome have a practical relevance for anyone who wants to help others to overcome a drink problem.

- ### Dependence and harm
  Alcohol Dependence Syndrome does not, as original definitions of alcoholism did, confuse dependence on alcohol and the harm caused by alcohol. Although they are often related, it is quite possible for someone to be dependent on alcohol without it having caused much harm in the physical, work and family aspects of his life. Equally, someone else may have suffered irreparable harm without having become dependent on alcohol.

  A good example of someone who can often be markedly dependent but relatively unscathed is the landlord. This is a particularly 'at risk' profession (see Chapter 4) because he can start drinking in the morning, ostensibly to taste the beer in the cellar, and can then continue to drink steadily through until closing time every day. He does not get very drunk, his wife works with him and all his drinks are bought by others. Under these circumstances, he has no major problems with his work, marriage or finances. On the other hand, it is possible to get alcohol related pancreatitis (a potentially fatal illness and therefore highly harmful) after a casual binge rather than from continued and long-term drinking. However, it is probably true to say that the more dependent a person becomes on alcohol, the more closely dependency and harm are correlated. This is demonstrated in Figure 3.

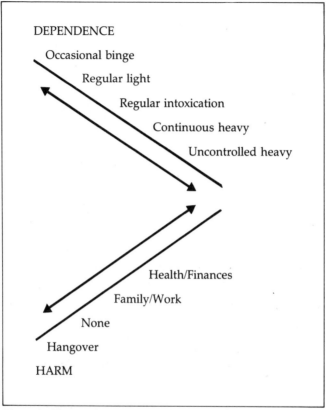

DEPENDENCE

Occasional binge

Regular light

Regular intoxication

Continuous heavy

Uncontrolled heavy

Health/Finances

Family/Work

None

Hangover

HARM

Figure 3: The correlation of dependence and harm

The Alcohol Dependence Syndrome argues that dependence and alcohol related harm should be separately identified and not confused. Whilst harmful consequences must be dealt with if possible, it is a reduction in dependency which is the ultimate aim of any treatment.

- **Flexibility**
  The Alcohol Dependence Syndrome allows for greater flexibility when deciding on a treatment goal. As discussed more fully in Chapter 9, it raises the possibility that total abstinence need not be the aim of treatment. If dependence is judged to be mild, it seems likely that controlled drinking and, ulti-

mately, social drinking may be a definite treatment possibility. If, on the other hand, dependence is severe, say if someone repeatedly fails to exert control over his drinking, it would probably be best to adopt an abstinence goal.

- ### Self-help
  By not implying an underlying disease state, Alcohol Dependence Syndrome subtly shifts the responsibility for a cure from the therapist to the patient. In practice this means that a person facing a drink problem cannot say, 'I can do nothing about my drinking: I have a disease'.

- ### Success and failure
  Alcohol Dependence Syndrome has far-reaching implications for the ways in which success or failure can be assessed. It seems fair to say if the severity of the syndrome has decreased and/or the amount of alcohol related harm has been reduced that this is, to a greater or lesser degree, a success.

  Success was previously a black and white issue. If a person was abstinent he was a success and if he had a drink he was a failure. An example from an American author highlights this danger. He recalls an AA member who had been totally abstinent for 20 years and so had achieved considerable status within his group. Unfortunately he had a brief two day drinking episode. The results of this slip were profound. He lost all recognition and status within the group. At his AA meetings he could not say, 'I am Joe and have been sober for 20 years,' but rather, 'I am Joe and have been sober for two weeks.' His abstinence for 20 years and his ability to stop drinking after two days went unrecognised. Finding appropriate ways of judging success is one of the most difficult problems in the field of alcohol dependence (see Chapter 11).

- ### Treatment
  Alcohol Dependence Syndrome suggests that not all 'alcoholics' are equally dependent on alcohol. The implication here is that the nature of the treatment offered to an 'alcoholic' should be determined by the degree of his dependence. It is probably true to say that until recently all 'alcoholics' were fitted to a treatment rather than the treatment fitted to their needs. Now, however, it is clear that all alcohol dependent people must be seen as individuals and offered treatment which is appropriate to their particular problem.

- **Amount consumed**

Of course, there is a correlation between how severely someone is dependent on alcohol and the amount of alcohol which actually passes between his lips. 'How much do you drink?' is one of the first questions asked of anyone with a drink problem. However, the amount drunk is not one of the more formal measures of severity of the Alcohol Dependence Syndrome and it can be seen as separate from dependence, although obviously related to it. Dependence is more concerned with state of mind and the ability to control drinking.

An example of why the amount consumed is not as important as it might appear is that of university students in general, and medical students in particular, who have a reputation for being heavy drinkers. It would not be considered abnormal for a medical student to consume a large number of pints over the weekend and, sometimes, during the week as well. However, that same medical student may eventually become a GP. If he were then to drink the same amounts as he did when he was a student, this would probably be considered abnormal. It is highly likely that drinking would be taking precedence over work and family, that he would be thinking about alcohol quite a lot and that the variability of his drinking habits would be less than in his student days. In short, he would not be considered very alcohol dependent as a student but, despite drinking the same amount, he would be regarded as quite dependent when a respected, middle-aged GP.

Some people then, could be assessed as quite dependent without necessarily drinking vast amounts and so, while the amount drunk and the degree of dependence are related, they are essentially separate issues.

The signs are that the implications of Alcohol Dependence Syndrome are beginning to affect the outlook of professional workers faced with the practical problems of helping very distressed fellow human beings. The fact that Alcohol Dependence Syndrome can be related to any model of alcoholism should help it gain even more acceptance in the future but it must be remembered that we are always gaining knowledge and that few things remain unchanged for long. Alcohol Dependence Syndrome is at best provisional and will undoubtedly be modified in the light of new knowledge and advances. One of its virtues is that it can incorporate change.

2 Alcohol – a health concern

Introduction

Probably no other so-called recreational drug can boast such a wide range of medical and psychological complications as alcohol. Although the percentage of drinkers running into health troubles is quite small, so many of us drink that the actual numbers are large and they make heavy demands on health services of all kinds.

If we use the definition of Alcohol Dependence Syndrome as it appears in the International Classification of Diseases (see page 21), between one in five and one in four patients in general hospital medical beds have an illness either caused directly by excessive drinking or in which drink has played a significant part. In general psychiatric hospitals, even more patients, about one in three, have a drink problem. This high figure is not surprising because alcohol is often taken to relieve psychological symptoms such as depression, lack of confidence and anxiety. Actual drinking problems can be so well masked that time and energy are wasted on treating a recurrent illness not obviously connected with excessive drinking. Dependents of problem drinkers are also known to be over-represented among those seeking medical help, possibly because of the stress of living with an 'alcoholic'.

If any improvement is to be made we need to develop our skills in recognising alcohol dependence in its earliest stages. Warning signs do exist and it is important that not only members of the health care teams but also members of other 'helping' professions such as social workers, counsellors, clergymen and the police should be able to recognise them. However, some parts of this chapter are intended solely for members of health care teams. For example, on no account should anyone other than a qualified practitioner prescribe drugs and all drugs should be taken only by the person for whom they were prescribed, for the reason they were prescribed and in the quantities they were prescribed.

Detecting a drink problem

Health care teams are in a privileged position to detect problem drinking because many patients with social, psychological or physical troubles which are related to drink often visit a doctor at an early stage, although often with seemingly unrelated complaints. There are also particular illnesses that should automatically alert a doctor, nurse or health visitor to enquire about drinking habits. Failure to detect problem drinking will almost certainly have long term consequences on a person's health and will also have repercussions on society. Short term costs to health services may also be considerable.

Possible consequences to health care services of failure to detect problem drinking

Recurrent attendances at the clinic and sometimes hospital admissions for trivial physical complaints

Inappropriate and expensive investigations for complaints such as chronic diarrhoea and seizures

Recurrent attendances at Outpatient and Accident and Emergency Departments often resulting in an overnight stay in hospital

Premature self-discharge from hospital

Unexpected acute illness, especially DTs (see page 43) during hospital stay

Development of serious physical or psychiatric illness requiring chronic care

Inappropriate prescription with harmful or fatal consequences

Inappropriate operative procedures for such conditions as peptic ulcers

Unexplained failure of treatment for anaemia, anxiety, etc.

Obstetric and paediatric failures such as abortion and foetal alcohol syndrome

---

Obviously, it would be inappropriate to ask everyone who came into contact with the health services about their drinking habits; no-one would think of asking someone with 'flu how much he drank. But it should be equally unthinkable not to ask a man who suffered from vomiting every Monday morning about his drinking. The suggestion is that a high level of suspicion is needed to detect problem drinking, but your enthusiasm should be tempered by some filtering system that selects out high risk cases; in other words, you need to bear a list of risk factors in mind.

Health at risk factors – Checklist

Clinical	'Alcoholic' appearance Smells of alcohol Frequently talks about drinking
'Alcoholic' symptoms	Withdrawal seizures (see page 37) Tremulous state (the shakes, see page 38) Tremulous and hallucinatory state (the horrors, see page 38) Fits (see page 42) Delirium tremens (see page 43) Amnesic spells (loss of memory) Tachycardia (increased heart rate)
Psychological illnesses	Depression (see page 45) Anxiety (see page 46)

	Dementia (see page 47)
	Wernicke-Korsakoff syndrome (see page 48)
	Morbid jealousy (see page 49)
	Self-poisoning
Physical illnesses	Gastritis (see page 51)
	Peptic ulcer (see page 51)
	Pancreatitis (see page 51)
	Fatty liver (see page 51)
	Hepatitis (see page 52)
	Cirrhosis of the liver (see page 52)
	Peripheral neuropathy (nerve damage, see page 53)
	Malnutrition (see page 54)
	Heart failure with an unknown cause (see page 54)
	Tuberculosis
	Recurrent infections
	Recurrent spontaneous abortions (see page 54)

These are all signs which should prompt the question, 'Do I suspect a drink problem?', but, before examining some of them in more detail, it is important to know something more of alcohol as a drug. What exactly is alcohol, how does the body break it down and what effects does it have on us?

What is alcohol? Alcohol as a drug

Alcohol is a drug that is taken mainly for its psychological effects. Basically, it depresses the nervous system and allows people to lose their inhibitions. This often means that they feel their conversation is more sparkling than usual, that they appear to be more confident and that they feel less tense. Man has enjoyed the effects of alcohol since he first tasted it. However, if a drug company discovered alcohol today there would be no chance at all of it receiving approval from a Drugs Safety Committee and it would never be marketed for human consumption.

- **Alcohol content in different drinks**
  Chemically, alcohol is a very simple substance – $C_2 H_5$ OH. It is produced by the action of yeast on sugars in various fruits and vegetables (a process known as fermentation) which can yield beverages with an alcohol content of up to 14% by volume. This means that 14% of the liquid is absolute alcohol. To make stronger drinks, the process of distillation concentrates the alcohol and it is theoretically possible to produce 100% alcohol, but most spirits designed for drinking such as whisky, vodka, brandy or gin, are 40–50% alcohol by volume (see Appendix 2).

  It is conventional to estimate alcohol intake in grams, and a detailed list of the alcohol content of different drinks can be found in Appendix 2, but the following estimates may be helpful.

½ pint of beer	10 grams
Single whisky or gin	10 grams
Glass of wine	10 grams
Glass of sherry or vermouth	10 grams

A daily intake of more than 100 grams is likely to damage health, especially in women (though, for some people, even less than this amount may cause damage).

As far as the risk of physical harm is concerned, it is the amount of actual alcohol consumed that is important and it is of little consequence whether it is taken as beer, sherry or vodka. Because the alcohol in spirits is concentrated, it may well be the case that someone who drinks spirits drinks more alcohol than a beer drinker (it is difficult to make two shorts last as long as a pint of beer). It may also be that spirits are more likely to cause stomach upsets than beers, but if you want to avoid serious health problems it is a myth that beer drinkers are safe and spirit drinkers are not.

Alcoholic drinks contain many other substances besides alcohol and water. These substances, called congeners, make up the taste, the colouring and bouquet that give a drink its individuality. Relatively little is known about congeners but they are large in number, often chemically complex, and have many ill-understood effects. Drinks such as red wine or brandy which contain a lot of congeners seem to cause worse 'hangovers' than purer drinks such as vodka. More significantly, it has been shown that performance at psychological tests which evaluate a person's continued ability to drive a car is impaired for a longer time after taking drinks with a high content of congeners than after taking purer drinks.

- ### How the body breaks down alcohol
  ### (the metabolism of alcohol)
  Alcohol is absorbed into the blood stream from the stomach and the intestines. All of the blood from the stomach and the intestines then passes through the liver before going into the general circulation. The peak blood alcohol level after drinking a pint of beer is reached after about an hour, but this may be delayed if there is food in the stomach. The strength of the drink also influences how quickly the alcohol is absorbed. Many heavy drinkers have found that an alcohol content of about 20% gives the most rapid absorption and their first drink is often a beer with a whisky 'chaser'.

  Once absorbed into the body, the alcohol is metabolised (broken down by the liver), first to acetaldehyde, a highly toxic chemical, which in its turn is quickly metabolised to acetic acid and then carbon dioxide and water. The rate at which alcohol is metabolised is remarkably constant regardless of a person's size or how regularly he drinks.

  The amount of alcohol in the blood is measured by the number of milligrams present in 100 millilitres of blood and this is usually abreviated to 'mg%'. For example, the maximum blood alcohol level permitted when driving a car in Great Britain is 80 mg%. The following figures may be helpful guidelines:

  10 grams of alcohol raise the blood alcohol level 15 mg%
  10 grams of alcohol are completely metabolised in one hour
  10 grams of alcohol contain 150 calories

  As an example, if someone drank 2 pints of beer, he could expect his blood alcohol level to reach 60 mg% after about an hour and it would take another three hours before all the alcohol was out of the body. Many people drive their cars some hours after drinking unaware that their blood alcohol level is in excess of the legal limit because they have not appreciated just how long it takes to 'burn off' alcohol. This

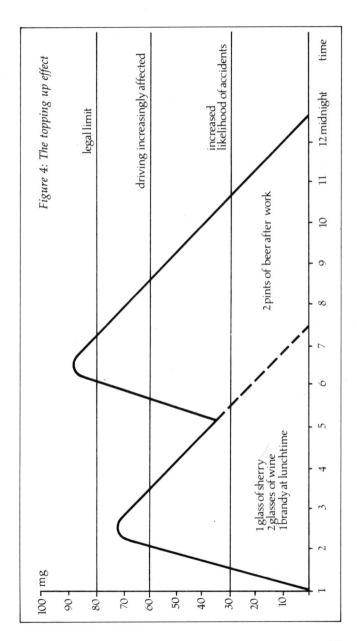

Figure 4: The topping up effect

35

can be illustrated by the 'topping up' effect that may occur with drinking at lunch time and then again in the early evening (see Figure 4).

- *The effects of alcohol*
  The immediate effects of drink are well known and include losing inhibitions, becoming more talkative, less self-conscious and probably feeling more cheerful. Alcohol, however, is not a stimulant drug but a depressant (a drug that dampens down the activity of the nervous system, rather like a tranquilliser).

  At a blood alcohol level of 80 mg% (about 2½ pints of beer or five singles of spirits) judgment is impaired, people are less responsive to what is going on around them, and the risk of a road traffic accident is twice that when sober. As the blood alcohol level rises to 150 mg% there is likely to be loss of self-control, possibly violence and a 25 fold increase in the risk of having a road traffic accident. At 200 mg% slurred speech, staggering and memory loss for subsequent events would be expected and at 500 mg% (the equivalent of drinking a bottle of spirits or about 15 pints of beer) death is possible. In general, regular heavy drinkers will be able to tolerate much higher blood alcohol levels than these. There is a case recorded of a Japanese 'alcoholic' who showed no signs of intoxication with a blood alcohol level of 480 mg%!

  These are some of the immediate effects which alcohol can have upon the body. The next three sections of this chapter move on to examine some of the consequences of excessive drinking outlined in the *Health at risk Checklist* on page 31. They are *psychological harm, physical harm* and, firstly, *withdrawal symptoms*, beginning with an experience many people are familiar with, a hangover.

Withdrawal symptoms

- *Hangover*
  A hangover is really nothing to do with withdrawal but is included here since it inevitably follows a heavy drinking session. Anyone who drinks can suffer from a hangover though, curiously, people who are markedly dependent on alcohol often say that they do not.

Still intoxicated
Dehydrated (alcohol is a diurectic, increasing the flow of urine)
Gastritis (nausea and loss of appetite, anorexia)
Effect of congeners (headache and 'not with it')

Apart from the obvious preventive measure of not drinking so much, there is probably no better cure for a hangover than a pint of water and a dose of a proprietary brand of effervescent salts, available without a prescription.

- **Withdrawal symptoms proper**
  As someone becomes used to drink he develops what is known as tolerance. This means that the body, and in particular the brain, has been exposed to alcohol so much that it has adapted itself accordingly and functions normally in the presence of alcohol. 'He can hold his drink', does not mean 'he' has any superior qualities to everyone else just that 'he' drinks regularly!

  Tolerance to alcohol can develop very rapidly and the degree of tolerance will depend on how much alcohol is drunk and how regularly. If someone is tolerant to alcohol and suddenly stops or substantially reduces his drinking he is likely to experience withdrawal symptoms. In fact what happens is that the brain, tolerant to alcohol, actually works better with alcohol in the system than without it and when the blood alcohol level falls, the brain, in the absence of the depressant effect of alcohol, becomes overactive. There are four distinct kinds of withdrawal states:

  Tremulous state
  Tremulous and hallucinatory states
  Fits
  Delirium tremens (DTs)

  Opinion is divided as to whether or not it is necessary for someone to be admitted to hospital if he goes into a tremulous or tremulous and hallucinatory state. With fits and delirium tremens (DTs) medical help must be sought. In any case, the rule should always be **if in doubt, get medical help**.

Tremulous state (the shakes)
This is the most common withdrawal state. The symptoms reach their most intense about 24 hours after reducing alcohol intake and the early, acute withdrawal phase is over within five days or so. Symptoms are not restricted to 'the shakes'. Indeed there are few symptoms, be they psychological such as 'irritability' or physical such as 'ringing in the ear' that may not form a part of the withdrawal process. Sometimes withdrawal symptoms are trivial and cause no distress, but they can be very severe and require treatment from a doctor or may be self-treated by taking another drink.

There are two unpleasant aspects to the tremulous state; mood changes such as anxiety and depression, and the physical effects such as 'a racing heart', which may in itself cause some anxiety. 'The shakes' can cause embarrassment in public and they are often so severe that they make it difficult to stop shaking for long enough to get the first drink of the day down as John and Sally found:

John
John is 46, his wife has left him, he is unemployed and is slowly drinking away his savings. He was seen one morning waiting for the pub to open. He was shaking all over and looked decidedly unwell. When he got into the bar he went to the far end hoping no-one would see that he had to bend down and drink his beer while the glass was still on the bar. His hands were so shaky that if he'd tried to lift a full glass most of the drink would have been spilled.

Sally
Sally is 34, and her husband died in a traffic accident three years ago though leaving her in a financially comfortable position. Sally stays in bed most of the day and only goes out in the early evening to the pub and the off-licence. She drinks a bottle of gin a day and has other drinks bought for her. She pours herself a large gin before going to sleep at night because she knows she will be too shaky to pour it in the morning. She pours it into a large tumbler so that it is not spilled when she picks it up.

Tremulous and hallucinatory states (the horrors)
Essentially, these are the same as 'the shakes' but there is also disturbance of vision. This is not usually frightening and does not amount to seeing things that are not there such as 'pink elephants'. There may be spots or flashes in front of the eyes

or distortion of real objects. For example, the wall may appear to bend in and out. Sometimes animals *are* seen, but usually the images are fleeting. People most commonly imagine small spider-like insects or animals such as rats. Ringing or buzzing in the ear may be a part of withdrawal but actually 'hearing voices' is not. Nightmares are quite common during withdrawal and are not to be confused with hallucinations which can only occur when someone is conscious, not asleep.

Whilst you need to be aware of the scope of common withdrawal symptoms, it is important to remember that many of them may be associated with other conditions. For instance, sleeping badly can also be a symptom of an anxiety state. This Checklist summarises the symptoms which are most specific to alcohol withdrawal.

Most specific alcohol withdrawal symptoms – Checklist

Whole body shakes
Face shakes
Hands shake
Cannot face the day
Panic
Guilt
Nausea
Visual hallucinations
Tiredness
Choking

How best to treat these withdrawal symptoms is a matter of some debate. Some specialists say that a person suffering from withdrawal should always be admitted to hospital and drugs used to cover the 'drying out' (the period during which the body readjusts itself to managing without alcohol). Other specialists believe that drugs should not be used and that the 'drying out' should take place away from hospital. However you decide to tackle the problem, always keep to these two guidelines:

● Remember to monitor the withdrawal phase.
● Remember that an explanation must be found if withdrawal is not over in 4–5 days.

Some kind of sedation is usually needed. This may simply mean being with someone and giving support by 'talking him through' the withdrawal. However, it is more common for sedative drugs to be given. A mixture of the two is best of all. Special charts are available to monitor the progress of withdrawal but common sense can be nearly as good. Two simple tests that anyone can do are to:

● Ask the patient to hold out his hands with the fingers spread and note how shaky they are.
● Take the pulse rate; if it is fast (say more than 100 beats per minute) this suggests significant withdrawal.

Add your general impression of how ill the person looks to these two tests and you have a very fair and reasonably objective assessment of how 'drying out' is going. These tests should be repeated at regular intervals and it is important that you **write down your observations**.

Withdrawal covered by drugs must have adequate medical supervision and, because of the possibility of drug/alcohol reaction, the patient should be kept well away from supplies of alcohol which he may be tempted to use. The decision as to whether or not to use drugs to cover withdrawal should be based on a doctor's assessment of the severity of withdrawal and on how severe he thinks withdrawal might be given the patient's past history. The drug chosen may well belong to a group of drugs called the benzodiazepines. Included in this group are *Valium, Librium, Ativan*, etc. The benzodiazepines have the advantage of a wider margin of safety than other tranquillisers. Quite large doses (*Valium* 20 mgm, *Librium* 50 mgm or *Ativan* 5 mgm, four times a day) may be appropriate and may initially need to be given by injection since inflammation of the stomach (gastritis) after heavy drinking will prevent drugs taken orally being absorbed properly. Whichever of these drugs is given, it should be tailed off to nothing **within five days**. Probably the most common mistake in the drug treatment of withdrawal is to underprescribe initially but to prescribe for too long.

Other drugs might be used to cover the withdrawal period. A group of drugs called phenothiazines which includes trade names such as *Largactil* and *Sparine* is sometimes used but may increase the risk of fits. There may be other possible side effects which most notably affect the liver and the regulation of blood pressure. Perhaps the best alternative to benzodiaze-pines then is a drug called chlormethiazole (*Heminevrin*). A disadvantage here is that, if the dosage recommendations are not followed, it may be difficult to wean patients off chlormethiazole.

It is usual and, arguably, mandatory to give vitamin sup-plements by injection to anyone in withdrawal until normal eating habits are restored. One time-honoured preparation is *Parentrovite* which contains vitamins of the B group and vit-amin C. The reason for giving this is that heavy drinkers often neglect their diet and may be depleted of essential vitamins. They are especially likely to be deficient in vitamin B_1 (thiamin) and at risk of developing the very serious condition, Wer-nicke's encephalopathy (see page 48).

Handling withdrawal symptoms pales into insignificance in the face of some of the medical and psychiatric problems that may co-exist with the withdrawal state. In particular, head injury and the abuse of other drugs should be borne in mind. Finding out about the abuse of other drugs is particularly important because they may be ones which produce a drug-alcohol reaction. Anyone who is being 'dried out' should have a thorough medical and psychiatric check, though this may not be possible either because the necessary resources are just not available or because the patient is in no state to allow such an examination. Most 'drying out' is uneventful and so it is all the more important to be alert for the one case where something is not quite right. What possibilities should be considered?

Medical problems co-existing with withdrawal states Checklist

Likely to be active at day 1
Head injury
Drug intoxication
Infection (especially pneumonia)
Heart failure
Liver failure
Hypoglycaemia (low blood sugar)
Fat embolism (blockage of a blood vessel)
Wernicke encephalopathy (see page 48)
Electrolyte imbalance (disorder of the chemical constituents of the body)

Psychiatric problems co-existing with withdrawal states
Checklist

Likely to be apparent after day 3
Anxiety state (see page 46)
Depressive state (see page 45)
Dependence on withdrawal medication
Confusional state from withdrawal medication
Delirium tremens
'Professional' patient

There is a lot of disagreement about where it is best to dry someone out and about whether 'drying out' or detoxification is of any use. Given adequately trained staff, 'where' probably matters very little except in monetary terms. What does matter is that the team who will be taking on later treatment and follow up will probably find it helpful, especially when it comes to gaining trust and confidence, to be involved at the start. The team may be a GP and community nurse, a Council on Alcoholism or an Addiction Unit. Exactly 'who' is unimportant as long as there is an early commitment to continued help from someone. The possibilities for home detoxification are always worth exploring in view of the benefits for the problem drinker, his/her family and friends, and of the reduced costs to health service resources.

Whatever the doubts of researchers, detoxification *is* the necessary beginning of any rehabilitation and workers in the alcohol field and many problem drinkers themselves would argue that 'drying out', in whatever way, is crucial to getting into active treatment. Even without plans for future treatment, detoxification is at the least a charity that should be afforded. It is also an inexpensive and appropriate alternative to prison for drunken offenders.

Fits (rum fits)
Fits are most likely to occur about 36 hours after reducing alcohol intake. The alcohol withdrawal fit is exactly like an epileptic *grand mal* seizure in that the patient falls to the ground unconscious, may turn a blue colour and twitch both arms and legs. A fit will last less than a minute and afterwards the patient may be confused about what has happened. Some-

times one fit is followed almost immediately by another and then another and this is known as *status epilepticus*. The fits most usually occur in runs of two to six at a time.

What to do if someone fits – Checklist

Prevent injury by moving the person to a clear space
Prevent the person biting his tongue by putting a knotted handkerchief (or something similar) between his teeth
When twitching stops lay the person on his left side and lift up the chin so he can breathe
Keep other people away
Do not put your fingers into the person's mouth
Do not use force to stop the twitching

If it is at all likely that a fit or fits are a consequence of withdrawal from alcohol, the person should be admitted to hospital. The reason for this is that more fits are likely and, in about a third of cases, fits herald delirium tremens.

Delirium tremens (DTs)
Delirium tremens, or DTs, is the most serious of withdrawal states. Even with hospital treatment about 15% of patients die. The beginning of DTs is usually delayed for two to three days after reducing alcohol intake.

Very often when people say they have had the DTs they have not at all. It may be bravado, it may be ignorance that leads them to say this but you should always check just what they mean.

Perhaps the central feature of delirium tremens is hallucinations, which are most commonly visual though they can be of touch or of hearing. Most typically rats, spiders or snakes are seen, often in vivid colours and moving threateningly towards the person. Sometimes a person may see Lilliputian figures which he finds amusing or he may see frightening distortions of real people or real scenes. The person is usually confused about the time of day, about the date and about where he is. He is over-active, easily distracted and it is virtually impossible to communicate with him. The body is in a state of over-arousal and the signs of this are a high temperature, sweating and a fast pulse. All cases of delirium tremens should be taken to hospital.

Whilst many cases of DTs abate within a day or two with only minimum sedation, others will require intensive nursing and medical care for as long as a week. Patients should be nursed in as constant an environment as possible. Avoid bright lights and bright coloured or patterned furnishings. In severe cases, very large doses of sedative drugs will be required and it will often be necessary to maintain adequate fluid intake by intravenous infusion.

Causes of death from delirium tremens – Checklist

Irreversible hypoglycaemia (low blood sugar)
Cardiovascular collapse (shock)
Malignant hyperthermia (uncontrollable high temperature)
Secondary infections (usually pneumonia)

Research has shown that clients of detoxification centres (see page 96) are not, for some reason, particularly prone to delirium tremens. This is surprising since it always used to be thought that it was the most hardened drinkers who suffered most from DTs. One possible explanation is that continued heavy drinking damages the brain, or parts of it, to such an extent that it is no longer capable of responses such as hallucinations. A simpler explanation may be that, contrary to popular belief, the single, homeless 'alcoholic' (see Chapter 6) does not in fact get very intoxicated although he drinks at a steady rate.

Psychological harm

Some of the psychological states that follow alcohol abuse such as depression and anxiety may be subtle, insidiously progressive and their link with alcohol may be obscure. Other conditions are more clearly to do with excessive drinking and these include dementia, Wernicke-Korsakoff psychosis, morbid jealousy and 'alcoholic' hallucinosis.

44

- *Depression*

Feels unhappy or sad
Feels hopeless
Tearful
Loss of energy
Loss of interests
Feels guilty
Self-blame
Gloomy about future
Suicidal thoughts
Loss of appetite
Sleep difficulties

Depression is probably one of the most difficult psychological states to assess. Many workers in the alcohol field have drawn attention to the relationship between alcoholism and depression but the difficulty is that the relationship is very complex. The depression may simply be a reaction to the disastrous life situation many problem drinkers get into, it may be part of withdrawal or it may be quite independent of the consequences of drink and could even be a cause of drinking.

Depression, which may or may not be the result of alcohol abuse, may be an internal cue for drinking. There is very clear evidence, particularly from studies of people suffering from manic-depressive psychosis, that a depressed mood is a very potent drinking cue.

A striking and most interesting aspect of depression in 'alcoholics' is the huge difference between how depressed 'alcoholics' think they are and how depressed professional workers assess them to be. On admission to hospital, as many as two thirds of 'alcoholic' patients see themselves to be significantly depressed and yet their doctors only diagnose one out of every ten of them as depressed.

Such a large discrepancy is hard to explain. Is there an unwitting lack of empathy towards patients known to be 'alcoholic'? Is there a tendency to regard a modest degree of depression as normal in patients who have run into the troubles typical of 'alcoholics'?

One clue may be in the association between drinking and self-destructive acts. Alcohol is a factor in about half of all overdoses. 15% of all suicides are committed by 'alcoholics' and suicide in 'alcoholics' is a staggering 40–50 times that of the general population. This could mean that the 'alcoholic's' perception of his mood is sometimes more accurate than the assessment made by those looking after him.

Depression really is a significant problem among 'alcoholics' and it is curious that more vigorous treatment has not been favoured even though research evidence shows that conventional treatment for depression with medication improves the chances of an 'alcoholic's' recovery. Some doctors may be reluctant to prescribe to 'alcoholics' because they feel that they will not take the tablets, that there is a risk of overdose and that the side-effects of some drugs may be compounded in 'alcoholics'. They may also consider that depression in problem drinkers is really to do with their life situation and will be unlikely to respond to medication. Failure to recognise and treat depression, however, risks an early return to heavy drinking and, perhaps, suicide. It may prevent a patient learning new skills which might be an important aspect of treatment.

- *Anxiety and panic attack*

Anxiety Checklist

Feels frightened
Feels tense
Worries about everything
Indecisive
Poor concentration
Sleep difficulty

Panic attack Checklist

Overwhelming fear
Escape from the situation
Feeling unreal
Fast pulse rate
Sweating
Difficulty in breathing

Like depression, anxiety can also be both a cause and an effect of drinking. It may be impossible to distinguish those symptoms of anxiety which are part of withdrawal from those which are part of a true anxiety state. There are two customary categories of anxiety: free-floating and phobic. With free-floating anxiety, the worry and anxiety are about anything and everything whilst with phobic anxiety there is more intense anxiety, often amounting to a panic attack, attached to particular objects or situations. For example, it may be a fear of heights, a fear of going out into crowded places (agoraphobia) or a fear of meeting other people (social phobia).

Symptoms of both agoraphobia and social phobia are very common in the general population and perhaps a third or more of all people is at least moderately affected. Many of these people use drink to relieve or avoid anxiety but unfortunately there comes a time when so much alcohol is being consumed that cutting down on drinking itself induces a withdrawal state and generates further anxiety. This vicious circle may also develop in someone who is not inherently anxious but who is drinking so much and so often as to experience withdrawal effects repeatedly.

- *Dementia*

Checklist

Short-term memory impaired
Intellectual capacity reduced
Coarsening of personality

Many heavy drinkers are aware that their thinking is not as good as it used to be although nothing seems obviously amiss even to their close friends and relatives. After a period of 'drying out' there is often a very definite recovery and patients will say things like, 'I can think more clearly now', or, 'My thoughts are more together'. While some amount of recovery occurs within just a week, improvement will continue for many months.

Brain scans of 'alcoholics' with no obvious signs of brain damage show a shrinkage of the brain exactly like that found with old age and it is reckoned that regular heavy drinking takes 10 years off an individual's intellectual life. In other words, instead of becoming senile at, say, 73 years the 'alcoholic' will show signs of senility at 63 years. Intellectual deterioration has been noted particularly in the ability to think in concepts and the ability to hold an idea in the mind. 'Alcoholics' also have a tendency to stick doggedly to an idea having once latched on to it. Short-term memory difficulties often improve to a surprising degree with prolonged sobriety.

Memory lapses or blackouts where a person cannot remember all or part of events that happened during a drinking bout are caused by high blood alcohol levels and do not indicate any brain damage.

- **Wernicke-Korsakoff syndrome**

Wernicke Checklist

Confused for time and place
Drowsy
Double vision
Unsteady gait

Korsakoff Checklist

Poor short-term memory
Confabulation (filling out memory gaps)
Misplacing events in time

The Wernicke syndrome is a nutritional disorder caused by lack of thiamin (vitamin B_1). The illness is not unique to 'alcoholics' but may arise in other conditions where thiamin is deficient and this happens particularly when there is persistent vomiting, as in pregnancy or with a blockage in the stomach. Wernicke syndrome is especially common in 'alcoholics' because they tend to neglect their diet and therefore have depleted stores of thiamin. The metabolism of alcohol also requires thiamin and a heavy drinking session will soon use up any stores of the vitamin that there may have been. The brain needs thiamin to function properly and without it the symptoms of the Wernicke Syndrome develop in a matter of hours. The syndrome is most unusual among psychiatric disorders in that it can be diagnosed by a blood test (pyruvate level is raised), is curable by giving intravenous thiamin, and is preventable. The Wernicke syndrome is **an emergency requiring immediate admission to hospital**. Failure to treat it early and vigorously may result in a form of permanent brain damage (Korsakoff syndrome) and this will invariably mean long term institutional care.

The Wernicke syndrome is all too easy to miss in someone who is drunk. The tell-tale sign is the double vision which is present in over 95% of cases. If the Wernicke syndrome progresses to a state of brain damage which is called Korsakoff's syndrome then a short-term memory problem is the outstanding feature and the confusion and double vision clear up. Patients with Korsakoff's syndrome tend to fill out their memory gaps, a process known as confabulation. For example, someone who really had a boiled egg for breakfast will relate, obviously convinced of the truth, the details of a much more exotic meal. Confabulation usually leans toward the grandiose and often turns out to concern something that actually did happen but at some time in the past.

- *Morbid jealousy*

Checklist

Belief of marital infidelity
Seeks to confirm infidelity
Violence

Jealousy is a normal emotion and a little is probably beneficial to a relationship. If one or both partners are jealous, it gives a boost to their other half's self-esteem. With the morbid, or pathological, jealousy which is common among cocaine sniffers and people with sensitive personalities as well as 'alcoholics', it is almost always the male who is jealous. This may happen in the setting of a poor marital relationship or of poor sexual performance and either of these may be caused by heavy drinking. Husbands will go to extreme and bizarre lengths to confirm their belief that their wife has been unfaithful. Examples of this behaviour are frequent 'phone calls to check on the wife's whereabouts or inspection of her underwear looking for semen. Extreme violence with cuts, bruises and broken bones is also common. Unfortunately, there is no very adequate treatment and wives are often reluctant either to leave their husbands or to take them to court.

- **Alcoholic hallucinosis**

Checklist

Auditory hallucinations of a threatening nature
Insight retained
Sleep disturbance

Alcoholic hallucinosis is not a withdrawal state. Unlike hallucinations associated with withdrawal, the hallucinations in this condition are of voices which are usually threatening, reprimanding or otherwise unpleasant. Sufferers usually realise what is happening and as a result there is a high risk of suicide. The condition is not threatening to health and normally lasts a few days to a few weeks.

Physical harm

There is no organ in the body which is immune to the effects of alcohol, but those exposed to the most alcohol, the gut and the liver, are the most likely to be damaged. Unlike social harm (see Chapter 3) and, to a lesser extent, psychological harm, physical damage can much more readily be related to the amount of alcohol drunk. A generous estimate of the safe amount to drink is five pints of beer or a third of a bottle of spirits daily for men and somewhat less for women. Whilst problem drinkers risk premature death for a variety of reasons other than ill health, notably accidents and suicide, they also risk dying young from illnesses not clearly related to alcohol consumption. In particular, it seems that the body's resistance to infections and cancers of all kinds is diminished.

The intention here is not to offer a detailed account of all alcohol related illnesses, but rather to mention briefly the more common illnesses and issues they raise.

- **Gastritis**

  Gastritis is an inflammation of the lining of the stomach. The usual symptoms are nausea and anorexia (loss of appetite). It is a harmless condition, although vomiting of blood may be alarming. Gastritis settles quickly provided the stomach is not exposed to the irritant effects of more alcohol. An inflamed stomach will not be able to absorb food or medicines properly.

- **Ulcers**

  It is not certain that ulcers of the lining of the gut (gastric or duodenal ulcers) are caused by drinking although they are certainly associated with it. The worry of ulcers is that they may either burst or bleed and require an emergency operation which the problem drinker is in poor shape to withstand. An ulcer is unlikely to heal as long as drinking and/or smoking continue.

- **Pancreatitis**

  Inflammation of the pancreas is a serious complication of alcoholism and the patient must be admitted to hospital. The leading symptoms (vomiting and abdominal pains) may not suggest the correct diagnosis in someone who is intoxicated and there may often be a delay in treatment. The number of cases of pancreatitis due to alcoholism seems to vary greatly from one country to another.

- **Liver disease**

  The link between liver disease and drinking is probably the most widely known and, clinically, it is the most important. There are three distinct kinds of liver disease:

  Fatty liver
  Hepatitis (inflammation of the liver)
  Cirrhosis (scarred and fibrous liver)

  Fatty liver
  Alcohol blocks the normal metabolism of fat in the liver so that during heavy drinking there is a kind of dumping of fatty materials which causes a swelling of the liver. People do not need to drink at all heavily for this to happen and the liver returns to normal when drinking stops. There are rarely any significant symptoms, though tests of liver function may be slightly abnormal. Alcohol also has an immediate effect on the metabolism of carbohydrates. It prevents the liver building

up stores of glycogen which are converted to glucose, the body's energy source. If blood levels of glucose fall too low, coma quickly follows. In most people, a temporary arrest of the process of storing glycogen to convert to glucose when needed does not matter but problem drinkers may halt the process for so long that they have minimal glycogen stores and therefore no energy reserve.

Hepatitis
Alcoholic hepatitis is a much more serious condition. The liver becomes enlarged and tender and the patient feels generally unwell, has a fever and is jaundiced (the skin and eyes are yellowed). It has been estimated that about one-third of all 'alcoholics' will develop hepatitis and one-third of these will go on to develop cirrhosis. In both hepatitis and cirrhosis there is destruction of liver cells which may be sufficiently severe to precipitate liver failure.

Cirrhosis
In cirrhosis, the liver cells that are destroyed are replaced by scar tissue. This is made up of fibrous bands which shrivel the liver and squash the remaining healthy cells. A further complication is that blood flowing from the gut into the liver is obstructed by the fibrous tissues. This causes back pressure in the veins from the gut that stretch up into the throat. These veins become dilated and are then called oesophageal varices. They are rather like varicose veins in that they can easily rupture and bleed profusely.

Why some people develop hepatitis or cirrhosis and others do not, although they seem to drink roughly the same amount, is not certain. The pattern of consumption is probably important and it is generally accepted that a very steady intake of alcohol is more harmful than occasional heavy drinking sessions. Possibly a more important factor is the connection between a certain tissue type and susceptibility to liver disease. It has been shown that the presence of the tissue type marker known as HLA B8 and absence of the tissue type marker HLA A28 is associated with a particularly severe reaction against liver cells. These reactions occur more often in women than in men, and it is worth noting that five years after first being diagnosed as suffering from liver cirrhosis only about one-third of women will still be alive whereas nearly three-quarters of men will still be alive. Continuous abstinence after diagnosis does not improve the outlook for women though it does to some degree for men.

- **Blood**
  Alcohol has a toxic effect on the bone marrow which manufactures red blood cells and the result is that cells are released before they are properly developed. These cells are larger than normal. A blood test, the Mean Corpuscular Volume (MCV), measures this and is a useful indicator of alcohol abuse. Anaemia is unusual in 'alcoholics'.

- **Peripheral neuropathy**
  This is the name given to damage of the long nerves in the arms and legs. It is a disorder affecting between 10–20% of problem drinkers and it affects the legs predominantly. Very often the damage is only detected by physical examination. The symptoms include weakness and tingling which may be mild in nature, but sometimes there are also muscle pains and 'burning feet' which can be very troublesome.

  It is not entirely clear what causes the toxic effect of alcohol on the nerves and what part is played by accompanying nutritional deficiencies. No specific nutritional disorder has been identified although vitamins of the B group are probably important (thiamin, pyridoxine, nicotinic acid). Even if drinking continues, there is usually an improvement when a proper diet is taken. Recovery is often incomplete but can be expected to continue over a period of several months.

- **Myopathy**
  This is a rare condition where there is a sudden swelling and tenderness of the muscles, especially around the shoulders and hips. Some of the muscle fibres are destroyed so that there may also be weakness, but recovery over a period of a month or two is usual if abstinence can be maintained.

- **Cerebellar syndrome**
  The cerebellum is the part of the brain responsible for co-ordinating body movements. When there is extensive damage to the nervous system the cerebellum is often affected as well. The cerebellar syndrome appears as an unsteadiness in walking, as if intoxicated. There may be some recovery if abstinence can be maintained.

- **Malnutrition**

  Most problem drinkers neglect their diet to some extent and many, at least in periods of continuous drinking, eat nothing at all. The net result is that stores of important materials such as vitamins, proteins and minerals become low. With the exception of thiamin deficiency in Wernicke's syndrome, it is not entirely certain what effect malnutrition has, save that the body has no reserves to respond to any insult it may suffer. Choosing the right drink gives protection from some deficiencies. For example, beer contains quite large amounts of iron and folic acid. The most useful way of preventing at least some conditions would be to supplement drinks with thiamin but the indelicate flavour of this vitamin rules this out.

- **Heart disease**

  The association between alcohol abuse and heart disease is well established. The toxic effect of alcohol on the heart muscle weakens its pumping action and may even cause congestive heart failure, which is a state characterised by shortness of breath, swelling of the ankles and blueness of the extremities. This kind of damage to the heart is called cardiomyopathy.

  Alcohol may also cause abnormalities in the rhythm of the heart. These are most often not of a serious nature, but a predisposition to serious ventricular dysrhythmia (a form of heart attack) has been inferred from the high incidence of sudden death in young adult 'alcoholics'.

- **Foetal alcohol syndrome (FAS)**

Checklist

  Prenatal growth deficiency
  Postnatal growth deficiency
  Failure to thrive
  Delayed developmental progress
  Low IQ
  Microcephaly (small head)
  Flattened face
  Cleft palate and hare lip
  Minor abnormalities of heart
  Squint
  Joint abnormalities
  Genito-urinary abnormalities

All these symptoms are not always present in foetal alcohol syndrome.

It is fairly widely accepted that drinking and pregnancy do not mix. Abortions and stillbirths are unexpectedly high among 'alcoholic' women and abnormalities have been found in live children born to women who drink heavily. The essence of the FAS is, firstly, slight or minimal brain damage together with an odd appearance to the head and face. Some authorities have gone so far as to say that 'damage to the foetus by chronic maternal alcoholism has been one of the most common recognisable causes of mental deficiency'. Brain damage has tremendous social implications because many of these children will have poor home circumstances and grow up competing with 'normal' children, they will be low achievers, they will not escape the cycle of social deprivation, and may well become problem drinkers themselves. However it has been suggested that the FAS may not in fact be caused by the damaging effects of alcohol on the growing foetus but rather by coincidental issues, notably poor nutrition and smoking.

What is not at all clear is how much alcohol can safely be drunk during pregnancy and whether or not any particular pattern of drinking is likely to be harmful. It might be expected that especially vulnerable times for the foetus would be the 12th to 18th weeks and the last third of pregnancy since these are the times that the brain tissue is most actively developing.

There is a temptation to ask, 'Why does anyone ever drink?' but history has shown that all societies through the ages have felt a need for mind altering experiences and these have usually been achieved by using psychoactive substances of which alcohol, despite its harmful effects, is arguably a good choice on the grounds of packaging and plasticity.

Packaging speaks for itself and is a reflection of our sophisticated use of alcohol. There are long drinks, short drinks, strong drinks, weak drinks, warm drinks, cold drinks, pretty-coloured drinks, colourless drinks and so on. Alcohol is available in wrappings that suit most palates and most occasions. A bonus of this level of sophistication is that the exact amount of alcohol in any drink is known.

Plasticity is a concept used when talking about drugs in general. A very plastic drug is one which has effects determined substantially by the surroundings in which it is taken and, to a much lesser degree, by the nature of the drug itself. An example of a high plasticity drug is LSD. The effects depend so much upon the mood, the place and the people who are around when it is taken. If the setting is wrong, the experience is a 'bad trip' and, because of this unpredictability, the popularity of very plastic drugs is limited. At the other end of the spectrum, drugs with very low plasticity such as amphetamines or heroin have an exactly predictable effect whenever or wherever they are taken. This may seem much more desirable but the snag is that there seems to be an inverse relationship between plasticity and addiction. LSD is not at all addictive but amphetamines and heroin are both highly addictive and so again the appeal of these two drugs is restricted. Alcohol and cannabis fall somewhere in the middle. Neither drug is particularly addictive and both have fairly, but not totally, predictable effects. For example, a few beers at a party are likely to foster well-being and animated conversation while wine with a dinner for two will often stimulate different emotions.

So, as psychoactive drugs and recreational substances go, alcohol is not too bad. To bring things into perspective, we need to remember that for every hundred people, ten will not drink at all, three might have trouble with their drinking and this may directly affect the lives of another twelve people. It still leaves seventy five people out of every hundred who drink, enjoy it and do no harm to themselves or to anyone else.

3 The problem drinker and the family

Introduction

Although the divorce rate for people with a drink problem is much higher than for the general population, up to about 60% of the people who agree to treatment for their alcoholism have a marriage which is still intact. An even higher percentage of those who do not seek treatment for their problem drinking is likely to be married or in a long-standing relationship.

Many 'alcoholics' then will have some sort of family commitment and there can be no doubt that their drink problem will have affected the whole family in some way.

Unfortunately, in most cases, the family as a whole is not involved when it comes to treatment for the problem drinker except, perhaps, in a token way. Only rarely is there formal family therapy and it is even rarer for a wider circle of friends and acquaintances to become involved in what is called 'network intervention'. This 'network intervention' means obtaining the co-operation and collaboration of such people as the owner of the off-licence (or whoever the 'alcoholic' bought his regular supplies from), a work-colleague and, say, members of the darts team, as well as the help of the family.

The attitude of some alcohol specialists is that although they agree that a drink problem can involve the whole family, such strategies as 'network intervention' take up a lot of time which could be used to help another person with a drink problem. In any case, they argue, is there anything to be gained from working with the family as well as with the problem drinker?

In one word, yes. There are four points to the reasoning behind that answer.

There seems to be fairly limited success from treating problem drinkers in isolation. Might it not be sensible to get help from people who are constantly close to them?

How the members of a family handle problem drinking together is arguably very important. If this is so, they could be helped to work at the situation in ways that would help all concerned.

If we see problem drinking as a learned behaviour pattern, (see page 19), then the way in which parents use alcohol assumes importance in detecting children at risk of alcoholism and perhaps other deviant behaviour in later years. This is because children learn many behaviours from their parents (see pages 198–201).

There is a moral, if not legal, responsibility to be satisfied that children are not directly at risk of violence or neglect.

'Alcoholics' are not a homogenous group and, although common themes have emerged between families and alcohol abuse, it has been a formidable task to establish them. This chapter will be looking in detail at some of these common themes but it is important to remember when making practical use of them that every family is different. What constitutes a real drinking problem for one family may be no problem at all for another; and a drink problem may be indicative of another, different problem. It is also important to remember that alcohol abuse does not respect social classes. Families from any walk of life can have an 'alcoholic' in them.

A drink problem in the family?

Checklist

The family as a whole
Denial, rationalisation and collusion (see page 61)
Poor family atmosphere (see page 61)
Unhappiness and anxiety (see page 61)
Repeated verbal and physical aggression (see page 64)
Constant tension and insecurity (see page 67)
Social isolation (see page 63)
Sense of inferiority (see page 71)
Serious financial hardship (see page 64)
Change in social contacts (see page 65)
Involvement of police and school authorities (see page 67)

The 'alcoholic' partner
Changes in behaviour patterns (see page 63)
Hides drinks (see page 62)
Denial of problem (see page 62)

Sexual indifference and infidelity (see page 64)
Violence towards partner/children (see page 64)
Low self-esteem (see page 67)

The 'non-alcoholic' partner
Denial and rationalisation (see page 62)
Assumes extra responsibilities (see page 63)
Sexual problems (see page 64)
Experiences violence or may be violent (see page 64)
Anxiety and depression (see page 67)
Change in behaviour patterns (see page 63)

The children
At risk of violence and neglect (see page 64)
Frequently absent parent (see page 61)
Take on added responsibilities (see page 63)
Truanting (see page 70)
Show anxiety, fear and insecurity (see page 70)
Behaviour disorders – tantrums, overactive, destructive
(see page 70)
Less likely to make friends (see page 70)
Underachievement at school (see page 71)
Distant from parent (see page 71)
Punished in negative ways – deprivation (see page 71)
Strong, but strained, bonds between brothers and sisters
(see page 72)

Whether your concern is personal, as a close relative or family friend, or professional, as someone who comes into contact with a wide range of families and family problems, going through the items on this checklist may help you to decide whether or not a member or members of a family could have a drink problem.

An inquiring but open mind is vital, though you should be extremely cautious with your findings. Although not all the items on the checklist need to be present for there to be a drink problem, just isolated items are no real indicator. If you do suspect a drink problem but you feel unqualified to deal with it you should refer to an appropriate agency listed in Appendix 1 who will be able to offer specialised help in confidence (see also Chapter 8).

If it is your partner, husband or wife who has a drinking

problem, you may find it helpful to turn to the section on coping strategies which begins on page 67.

Problem drinking, stress and the family system

- ### Alcohol as a stress factor

An interesting and useful way of thinking about the effect of alcohol abuse on families is to consider alcohol as something which causes stress in a family in just the same way that a bereavement or even something pleasant, such as a summer holiday, causes stress. In fact, alcohol abuse can be a very powerful stress factor and can cause both long and short term damage to the wellbeing of the family.

Aspects of alcohol related family stress

Denial, rationalisation and collusion with drinking
Poor family atmosphere
Social isolation
Change in family behaviour patterns
Financial hardship
Sexual indifference and infidelity
Violence

Denial, rationalisation and collusion
Probably the earliest sign of alcohol causing stress in a family is the realisation that something is wrong but being unable to identify exactly what it is.

It is easy to imagine how alcohol can intrude into a happy family life. The sequence of events might begin when the husband stops off at the 'local' on the way home to 'talk about business'. Insidiously, he begins to do this frequently and starts missing the odd evening meal. Sometimes he does not get home until closing time and Mummy has to make excuses to the children for Daddy not being there to tuck them into bed. All this leads to a prolonged series of arguments.

The complementary sequence might begin when a wife who does not work outside the home meets friends for lunch and has a drink or two. She starts drinking every lunch time, even alone at home, and jobs around the house are missed. Later, she begins drinking in the afternoon and one day she forgets to meet the children from school. On occasions there is no evening meal when her husband gets home. Again, this leads to a series of arguments. There are obviously many other ways in which problem drinking can creep into family affairs.

The time it takes before the drink problem comes out into the open can be surprisingly long. One reason for this is that the problem drinker is a master of deception and concealment. Places in which drink is hidden are often sources of amusement after the event. Well known places are in the wardrobe, in a compartment in the car or behind the rubber plant. More adventurous concealers were the dentist who kept his whisky in his drill equipment and the housewife who kept her gin chilled under the gravel in the fish tank!

The second reason that problem drinking in a family is hidden for so long, particularly from outsiders, centres on denial. Denial operates in two ways. Firstly there is the situation where it would be too embarassing and shameful to admit to a drink problem in the family. This is particularly true when it is the mother who is drinking. Social conditioning has led us to see the mother as the key person responsible for bringing up the children and it is not really socially acceptable for women to be seen to be drunk. This means that there are at least two powerful reasons to deny that a woman is drinking heavily.

Whether it is the husband or the wife who drinks, myths about what 'alcoholics' are like and the sorts of people they are, the social stigma of being labelled an 'alcoholic', and the low expectations from any treatment offered probably contribute to the 'cover-up'. The denial is often bizarre in its absurdity and often puzzles the children who are dragged into what ultimately becomes a pretence.

Rationalisations by a partner for drunken behaviour in front of either acquaintances or other members of the family can become an easy way out of a difficult situation, although they wear thin rather quickly. Some of the more common ones are:

He's had a hard day
She hasn't eaten all day
He'll never grow up
I've told you drink and tablets don't mix!

In some cases, denial and pretence can operate in another way. It is obvious to someone outside the family that drink is a problem but the whole family itself denies it. This type of collusion or conspiracy suggests that members of a family see something terrible happening to the family system if the drink problem is admitted and something is done about it; in other words, family members have a vested interest in keeping the 'alcoholic' drinking.

Social isolation
The process of social isolation may be very gradual and can be minimal when a family mixes with groups where heavy drinking and normally unacceptable behaviour are tolerated. However, more often than not, embarrassment at having to make feeble excuses everywhere they go may lead a couple to turn down invitations. At the same time, it may well be that the number of enthusiastic invitations from friends and neighbours is dwindling. Families often become known for their involvement with the police or social services and the stigma tends to turn others away. Everyone has a limit to his/her tolerance of drunken behaviour.

Change in family behaviour patterns
The way in which rules in a family have to change because one member is drinking tends to depend upon the family but some general points can be made. Whichever partner drinks, the other will often find himself or herself taking on new and sometimes demanding responsibilities.

A husband may have to do the housework and the family shopping whilst a wife may have to take a responsibility for family finances and earning money. Their roles in the family change completely.

The children too must make changes, especially if it is the mother who is drinking. Usually the children take on responsibilities before they would normally do so. These may be fairly trivial chores such as doing the shopping, cooking meals and so on. Some people may argue that it is beneficial to cope with these tasks at an early age but other tasks such as looking after younger brothers and sisters or making excuses for drinking to friends and neighbours or to employers may be damaging.

These role changes are an almost inevitable and immediate consequence of someone in the family abusing alcohol.

Financial hardship

Drinking is an expensive hobby and, even for the better off family, it is not difficult to imagine other, better ways of spending the money. Compared with friends (or ex-friends) the family will feel inferior. They will not go for such exotic holidays, they will not have such a luxurious car and they probably will not have so many new clothes. Worse off families, perhaps where social security is the only source of income, will become deprived. Bills will go unpaid, there will be a temptation to steal or to encourage the children to do so, there will be a lack of food and heating in the home and the house will be neglected.

However, serious financial hardship is not inevitable and some 'alcoholics' set aside a fixed sum from their income for family expenses with almost religious zeal. Perhaps, having done so, they do not feel guilty about drinking what is left!

Sexual indifference and infidelity

Sexual activity is a fair guide to marital harmony and togetherness, and a waning of sexual interest usually reflects troubles in a relationship that are only rarely primarily of a sexual kind. A drink problem, which may itself simply reflect relationship problems, often accelerates sexual disinterest that already exists and can actually be the cause of the disinterest. If the husband is the problem drinker, he may have extramarital sexual partners and boast about them to his wife, he may make excessive and, to his wife, offensive sexual demands when intoxicated. In some cases, he may lose sexual interest and become impotent even when sober.

In the face of an unloving or non-existent sexual relationship, the wife may satisfy her own sexual needs with another man. If the wife who stays at home is the problem drinker, she will probably have less opportunity to be promiscuous and to indulge in extra-marital sex than would be the case for a husband or wife who goes out to work. As with a drink problem, there is often a wish to talk about sexual problems in families but a shyness at doing so. One way into the subject might be a question such as 'Do you both sleep in the same bedroom?'

Violence

The constant threat of violence in a home is an intense source of family stress and episodes of verbal as well as physical aggression can indicate an underlying drink problem. The dilemma for anyone who tries to help is that the more violence there is, the more difficult it will be to treat the problem drinker effectively. In general, violent people experienced violence in their own childhood and it seems difficult to break the cycle and to prevent these people passing on violent behaviour patterns to their children.

There is a link between some incidents of child abuse and heavy drinking, and more than half of all wife beaters are also heavy drinkers. In cases like these, the pattern of drinking is important because it is drunkenness rather than steady drinking which is most often associated with violence. The risks of very serious injury are high if the violence stems from morbid jealousy (see page 49).

Violence does not always come from drunken men. Sometimes drunken women become violent, though this does not often happen in the home. Violence can also be directed at drunken wives by their partner.

- ### The family system
  The effects of stress on a family in which someone has a drink problem will be wide and diverse. To try and see clearly what is happening, it is often helpful to map out a family and its social contacts in a schematic way. In Figure 5, the family is shown as it might have been at one time, with two sets of social contacts, 'the pub' and 'the friends'. The ways in which the circles overlap show that:

Going to the pub is part of family life ('pub' circle overlaps 'family' circle).

Seeing friends is an important family activity ('friends' circle overlaps 'family' circle).

Seeing friends in the pub is part of family leisure activity (all three circles overlap).

An endless range of contacts could be included in the diagram but it is best to stick to those which seem most relevant to a particular family. Possible contacts could include work, school, church, evening classes and whatever social groups the family has dealings with.

By using this kind of diagram it is easy to get clear in your mind exactly what is going on in a family. Looking at Figures 5 and 6 together it is possible to see how drinking might

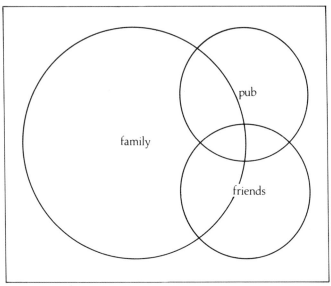

Figure 5: Family circles (i)

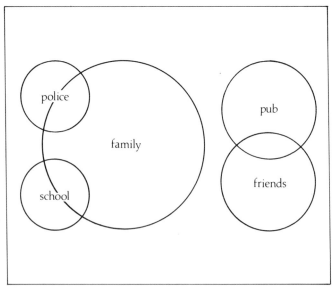

Figure 6: Family circles (i)

change a family's social systems. Two of the circles in Figure 6 still represent 'the pub' and 'the friends' but they no longer have anything to do with the family. Some new contacts have become major parts of family life. The police have become involved, possibly because of frequent noisy arguments in the home with calls from concerned or annoyed neighbours. School has also become an important contact, possibly because the children have started truanting or being destructive. The possibilities are endless and the intention here has been to offer just one example of how stress caused by problem drinking can upset a family system.

The effects of problem drinking on particular family members

Accepting the idea that alcoholism causes stress within a family, similarities can be found with the way a family reacts to other kinds of stress such as pregnancy or physical illness. In all these cases, the partner who is not affected tends to display symptoms of anxiety and depression. The loss of sexual interest also appears to be a common stress response and opting out of family decisions is not particular to the 'alcoholic'. It has been suggested that the role of alcohol in unhappy marriages has been over-emphasised and that couples who are dissatisfied with their situation are people who always were discontented and always will be. They see both themselves and their partner in an unfavourable light and describe each other with such adjectives as quarrelling, exploitive, unreliable and mistrustful. In short, though, whatever causes a family's troubles, whether it is alcohol or something else, the effects on the various members of the family can be very similar.

- ### The coping strategies of wives
As the husband indulges in excessive drinking, other members of the family need to adapt and so they behave differently. This is often true in the case of wives. Irene is an example of someone who had to learn to cope.

Irene
Irene was 42 years old and married to an Irishman who was generally seen as a hopeless case. He belonged to the drinking gang

on his estate, was often violent when drunk and invariably filthy in his habits around the home. Irene found work at a local bottling factory on the late shift and stayed at a male friend's house at night. Publicly, she said that this was only a 'friendly' relationship but in fact there was sexual involvement.

Irene's behaviour can be seen not only as a role change (see page 63) but also as what is called a coping strategy.

Initially, she had to get a job to keep the family together at all but, although she found the work difficult to begin with, she had made a successful role change; she had become the family breadwinner instead of her husband.

As it turned out however, this role change to breadwinner also became a coping strategy because Irene preferred to avoid her home in the evening. In fact, she preferred it so much so that she extended her avoidance behaviour to staying out all night, every night.

From the point of view of her husband's drinking, the fact that Irene began a sexual relationship with her friend would make any attempt to deal with the problem very difficult. In addition, this new relationship has taken on many of the functions of a marriage for Irene and has enabled her to cope better and with less stress.

The more aggression that a husband displays then the more bizarre and more various are the coping strategies that a wife will adopt. She is more likely to get drunk herself, to return hostilities, to lock her husband out and to seek separation or divorce. The more she has to cope with, the more coping strategies she draws upon.

Common coping strategies of wives of 'alcoholics' Checklist

Denial, rationalisation, pretence	or	Confrontation
Collusion with drinking	or	Action against drink
Avoidance/withdrawal	or	Attempts to control drinking
Marital breakdown	or	Marital reorganisation

Denial and rationalisation have already been discussed when looking at how alcohol causes stress but denial often merges into pretence when it has become clear to everybody concerned that drink is causing problems. This coping strategy rests on a forlorn hope that, 'time will heal everything if we just pretend things are OK'.

Confrontation is a better coping style. A wife should aim to have her husband agree about his drinking habits, to encourage him to discuss the ill effects of alcohol on himself and on the family or, in short, to be forceful in demonstrating the bad side of drinking to him. It may then be possible to reach an agreement on some sort of treatment.

There may be many reasons for *collusion with drinking*. For example, if the husband recovered the wife would no longer have reason to go out to work, the husband may be dull and boring when sober but fun and exciting when drunk, or there may be a lover who would have to go.

Taking *action against drink* is much more likely to cut back drinking. A wife must just pour drink away, ban alcohol from the house and take care not to be oversympathetic when her husband is drunk.

Avoidance and withdrawal from the relationship are often coping strategies that happen when there is a feeling of helplessness. A wife will keep out of the way, move to a separate bedroom, keep the children out of the way and not say anything for fear of reprisals.

The better strategy is to work actively on ways that might *control a husband's drinking*. She could fight back, make him jealous, go drinking with him or get drunk herself.

If there is no favourable change in a husband's drinking habits and no satisfactory coping strategy, even such as avoidance, has been found, then *separation or divorce* is likely to be seen as the sensible solution and it certainly may well be the best solution for the family as a whole.

A better hope for the family is that the wife will be able to *reorganise the family* excluding her husband but not severing all ties with him. This strategy leaves open the possibility of the family getting back together at a later date.

It is most important to remember that the coping strategies

most likely to have a desirable effect on a husband's drinking, though not necessarily the most comfortable ones, are those which **do not threaten the man but do threaten the drink**.

- *The coping strategies of husbands*
There has been very little study of the ways in which a husband reacts to an 'alcoholic' wife. One impression is that a husband denies the problem for much longer than a wife, but that, when it comes into the open, he is more likely to leave his wife than a wife is to leave her husband.

  Why men should find it so hard to accept that their wife has a drink problem is not at all clear. It could be that men are vain enough to believe it reflects badly upon themselves to have chosen a partner with a weakness for the bottle or perhaps it is simply the social disgrace that female 'alcoholics' seem to be burdened with. Even when a husband has had to admit that drink is the issue, he can put up a very serious resistance to his wife receiving treatment. He will search endlessly for a more agreeable 'diagnosis' and will settle for any 'label' other than 'alcoholic'. Anyone trying to offer treatment will often use up a lot of patience before it is accepted.

  Because drinking patterns are rather different for men and women, it may well be that a husband's coping strategies will differ a little from a wife's. However, there is every reason to suppose that the husband's behaviour most likely to alter drinking habits favourably will be similar to those outlined for a wife in the right-hand column of the Checklist on page 68. They are those which **do not threaten the woman but do threaten the drink**.

- *The effects of problem drinking on children*
Almost two thirds of child abuse or child neglect cases involve parents who have a drink problem. It is estimated that almost one third of children who have an 'alcoholic' parent will show signs of emotional disturbance such as anxiety, fear, feelings of insecurity and being unloved as well as anger and puzzlement as to why their family is different from others. About two thirds of the children of 'alcoholics' will suffer behaviour disorders such as truanting from school, tantrums, being destructive and being overactive.

  The children of 'alcoholics' are less likely to make friends, partly because their families have been rejected by 'non-alcoholic' families and partly because they are often psychologically disturbed anyway. There is also a risk of underachievement at school and of the children themselves becoming 'alcoholics' when they grow up. When asked about how they see their family, the children of 'alcoholics' tend to talk about the aggression associated with drinking and the family's social isolation. They tend to express disgust and shame about their drinking parent as well as a sense of not being liked by other families and of being different to them. They distance themselves from the drinking parent, perhaps because of fear, or perhaps because they never know what response they will get. The children may also distance themselves from the non-drinking parent, possibly because this parent has to cope for the whole family and so is often short-tempered and pressed for time.

Whilst over 80% of children under the age of 16 in 'alcoholic' families say they will never drink, the truth is that with one 'alcoholic' parent there is about a one in four chance of a child also becoming an 'alcoholic'. Another research finding is that the last born child of either sex, especially in larger 'alcoholic' families, is the one most likely to develop a drink problem.

In later adolescence, the children of 'alcoholics' may turn to alcohol abuse themselves, as well as to other generally unacceptable behaviour such as sexual promiscuity, drug taking and aggression. These delinquent behaviours seem to be a good indicator that alcoholism will become a problem in adult life. It is difficult to say exactly why these particular young adults should become involved in such behaviours but one reason could be that particular aspects of parenting which are common in 'alcoholic' parents are somehow related to delinquency and so lead to a high risk of alcoholism in adulthood. These aspects of parenting are to do with being uncaring and rejecting, being uninvolved in family matters, generating tensions and using deprivation as the sole method of child discipline. It could also be that some children of 'alcoholics' forget about the association between alcohol, aggression and unhappiness when they find out about the more desirable aspects of drinking. Another possibility is that there were no clear and unambiguous parental values in childhood and so other influences such as advertising and pressure from friends are much more powerful than normal.

However, it must be remembered that not all the children of 'alcoholics' will grow up to be 'alcoholics' themselves. No-one should ever assume that they will.

Family therapy

Research has shown that problem drinkers who have a stable family relationship are the most likely to benefit from some kind of help, and when so many problem drinkers do live in a close family setting it is perhaps surprising that family therapy finds very limited favour as a treatment for alcoholism.

Before considering family therapy in more detail, it may be helpful to look at the relationships within a family by using similar diagrams to those used earlier in this chapter. In Figure 7, a normal family is represented by strong boundaries around the whole family, with a close bond between mother and father, and, to a lesser extent, between mother and daughter and father and son.

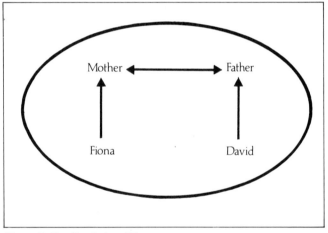

Figure 7: Family circles: (ii)

If the father develops a drinking problem as shown in Figure 8, everything is totally disrupted. The family boundary is weakened and excludes the drinking father, bonds between mother and father are lost and each now has a closer bond outside the family, the children have distanced themselves from both parents and, although the bonding between the children is strong, it is strained because Fiona is satisfying some of her needs for love and affection by 'mothering' David.

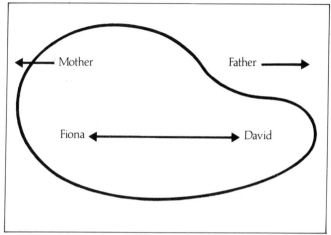

Figure 8: Family circles: (ii)

It invariably aids helpers to clear their thoughts by drawing the family system in this kind of way. Some concentrated thinking about the communications that are going on inside a family can make the aims of family therapy apparent. So, if it is all so simple, why not use this approach more often? The fundamental issue is timing.

For family therapy to work all the participants must accept the general idea and have some kind of commitment to it. Unfortunately, this does not happen very often in families which include a problem drinker. If the drinking husband or wife is denying the problem, time may be better spent with the non-drinking partner; if the drinker has been cut off by the family, there is no alternative but to engage in individual work; if the children are in care or with relatives, they may not be able to attend the treatment sessions.

There are many other issues. Is a co-helper needed? Does the family want to work in this way? Are workers happy to involve children in sessions where sex and drink may be prominent issues? Is a therapeutic relationship possible when a helper may need to take children into care? On a more optimistic note, a study of a family's social systems as in Figures 5–8 may indicate people in the extended family or outside the family who could be involved in therapy and cut out some of the problems of initiating family work with 'alcoholics'. Further reading on working with families can be found in Appendix 3. Of course, there are alternatives to family therapy and some of these are discussed in Chapters 8–10.

Alcoholism and the family is a complex subject but it is possible to draw out one or two threads. Firstly, if the stress which problem drinking is causing within a family can be removed or diminished, it will still take a lot of work to restore 'normality'. The partner who does not have a drink problem may be particularly resistant to this final readjustment; perhaps he or she feels reluctant to readjust the role changes that have just given new status and satisfaction. Secondly, even if the alcohol issue is resolved, there may well remain a family with abnormal relationships which never had anything to do with alcohol. Thirdly, the children of 'alcoholics' are likely to have some long-lasting psychological disturbances. If they are delinquent teenagers, they are very likely to become 'alcoholics' themselves in adult life. Fourthly, using diagrams such as those in Figures 5–8 can help to make it easier to think about ways of helping the 'alcoholic' family. For instance, you may think of some way of working which, even though it does not help the drinking parent, is a real benefit for the non-drinking members of the family.

Finally, it may be helpful to think about the aspects of family life which make success more likely, such as the ability of parents to share in decision making and household tasks, and a low level of hostility. A reasonable family atmosphere, a 'non alcoholic' partner who uses few coping strategies and is relatively free of anxiety and depression are all signs that therapy will be successful. However, very few 'alcoholic' families are so well-adjusted as this and therapy will often consume a great deal of time, skill, energy and above all patience.

4 Drinking and work

Introduction

Twenty years ago most employers scarcely recognised 'alcoholism' as a significant problem. There were stories of odd characters who were known as heavy drinkers but they were thought to be very few and far between and they could be tolerated until a suitable opportunity arose to dismiss them or to retire them on the grounds of ill health. As a general rule, however, the attitude of management was that they did not employ 'alcoholics'. The only work an 'alcoholic' was supposed to find was doing such tasks as labouring, cleaning and washing-up. These were the jobs no-one else wanted. It all reinforced the idea of the 'alcoholic' as male, single, bordering on the down and out, and with nowhere to go.

Twenty years on, attitudes are changing and more employers are beginning to realise that if most people in Great Britain drink and a certain number of them have a drink problem, then a proportion of the people they employ will inevitably have a drink problem as well. Employers are also beginning to realise that at some time this will have an effect on attendance, efficiency and safety.

Pubs and clubs, particularly in city centres, fill up at lunch time with people entertaining customers or colleagues, with leaving parties, birthday parties, and friends having a lunch time 'jar'. Most of these people will have to return to work and it is certain that some of them will have had 'a few too many'. It does not take a lot of imagination to realise that some will have 'a few too many' as a regular part of their lunch. Drinking and employment has recently been the subject of research which has shown that:

- The more alcohol we consume, the more likely we are to have problems related to drinking.

- Probably over 75% of problem drinkers are in employment.

- Problem drinking can cause very high levels of absence from work. Some studies have indicated that this can be in excess of 100 working days in the year leading up to treatment for alcoholism.

- Having a job helps an 'alcoholic' respond successfully to treatment.

The first three points suggest that it would be worthwhile developing more programmes for dealing with problem drinking in the work place and the fourth indicates that the results of such programmes are likely to be positive. Certainly, incentives like keeping a job, status and income enhance the prospects of a successful recovery for an employee who is a problem drinker. There are also incentives for the employer who will often have invested substantial sums in recruiting and training his workforce, and who has an interest in achieving a profitable return on his investments.

Inappropriate drinking at work

The difficulties alcohol can cause at work are not confined to employees who have developed long-term drinking problems which need some form of immediate treatment. Any employee who drinks in a way which affects his work is drinking inappropriately. People often drink inappropriately because they do not know enough about the properties of alcohol and its physiological effect. An example of someone like this is the shift worker who has to be at work at seven o'clock in the evening. His social life is disrupted by working shifts so he goes to the pub at lunch time and drinks six pints of beer between one and three o'clock. By the time he starts work in the evening his blood alcohol level is still too high for him to be driving and his reactions will be far too slow for operating high-speed machinery with any degree of safety. He is at least five times more likely to have an accident at work than someone who does not drink.

It is important that employees should know about the dangers of inappropriate drinking both before coming to work and during the working day. It reduces efficiency, productivity and safety standards, and it can also lead to arguments between colleagues and even physical violence.

'At risk' occupations

Whilst problem drinking is a risk in any job, there is evidence to suggest that certain occupations have a much higher risk of heavy drinking than others. Several factors are involved.

- *Availability*

  For many people, alcohol is readily available at work and these occupations often attract people who are fairly heavy drinkers already. At risk through availability are people who work in:

  Catering
  Hotels
  Public houses
  The brewing industry
  Retail alcohol sales

- *Mobility*

  Many people have to travel on business a great deal. This puts them at risk because they are separated from family and friends, and having a drink is a good way to get to know new people both professionally and socially. Two other reasons for heavy drinking could be the low cost of alcohol in many countries and the financial help given by subsistence and expenses. At risk occupations in this case are:

  Representatives and salesmen
  Sales engineers
  Maintenance workers
  Actors and entertainers
  Construction workers

- *Business entertaining*

  Most people agree that alcohol is a sign of hospitality and like to have a drink with a meal when entertaining. The restaurant or public house is often seen as a pleasant place to get to know customers, to discuss business with them in a less formal setting and to introduce them to colleagues and friends. Occupations at risk here include:

  Company directors
  Senior management
  (Export) sales staff
  Journalists

- *Social pressure to drink*

  Certain occupations have a 'tradition' of drinking and people working in them are often encouraged to drink as part of their social life. Sometimes, heavy drinking is seen as a way of becoming accepted in such occupational groups as:

(Merchant) navy
Armed forces
Journalists
Medical practitioners and students
Coal miners

- **Freedom and low supervision**
  Some occupations are relatively unstructured in terms of time keeping. Some people are able to work, to a certain extent, as and when they like. They are often accountable only to themselves and their job will have a sufficiently high status to allow them to cover up heavy drinking and the poor work performance which can result. Included in this category are:

Company directors
Agents
Lawyers
Doctors
Salesmen
Freelance workers
Journalists

However, it is true to say that many people who work in these at risk occupations realise their vulnerability and either do not drink at all when working (drinking at work is forbidden in some cases) or monitor their drinking very carefully.

Identifying the problem drinker

Although people who work in certain occupations (as outlined in the previous section) are particularly vulnerable to problem drinking, most industries and professions contain at least their fair share of heavy drinkers. It is important that personnel and welfare staff, as well as management, should be aware of possible problem drinkers. However, it is often close friends, colleagues or line managers who are the first to suspect that it is heavy drinking which is affecting someone's work performance. The checklist which follows should help to decide whether or not the suspicion is correct, though it is important to keep an open mind at all times.

You can apply this checklist when you feel that someone is not coming up to expectations in his work. It evaluates general work performance and should not be used by itself to decide whether or not someone has a drink problem. If you feel that drinking could be the cause of the problem after going through it you should go on to Checklist 2.

Uncertified absences
Certified absences
Low productivity
Unpunctuality
Time spent away from desk/workbench etc.
Lethargic
Bad tempered
Fluctuation of mood
Regular visits to occupational nurse
Reluctant to accept authority
Poor relationships with colleagues
Avoided by colleagues

Checklist 2

You can apply this Checklist to identify possible problem drinkers. If you feel that drinking could be the cause of the problem after going through it, go on to Checklist 3.

Uncertified absences – poor excuses
Certified absences – see Checklist 3
Lowered work performance
Accidents at work
Time spent away from desk/workbench etc.
Lethargic, depressed
Bad tempered
Fluctuation of mood
Drinking before work ⎤
Drinking at lunchtime ⎥
Drinking at work ⎥ Smelling of drink
Shaky hands ⎥
Flushed face ⎦
Avoided by colleagues
Requests for advances of pay
Borrowing money from colleagues

If all absences from work have been uncertified, the only course of action left is an interview with the person you suspect may have a drink problem, though you must not be surprised to receive a strong denial (see page 128). If absences have been certified you can apply this third Checklist to the reasons given for absence which may indicate a drink problem.

High suspicion of drink problem
Certification for any of these conditions can indicate a drink problem as there are close connections with heavy drinking.

Gastritis
Abdominal pain
Gastroenteritis
Peptic ulcer
Gastric ulcer
Duodenal ulcer
Cirrhosis

Medium suspicion of drink problem
The illnesses here may suggest a drink problem though people who do not drink heavily can also suffer from these conditions.

Diaorrhea
Indigestion
Food poisoning
Anxiety
Nervous debility
Depression
Hepatitis

Low suspicion of drink problem
The conditions here should be considered but do not necessarily indicate a drink problem.

Bronchitis
Lower back pain
Pancreatitis
Phobia

The next step

When a problem drinker has been positively identified using the Checklists, the dilemma faced by an employer is how to tackle the problem. Sometimes the problem drinker can control his own drinking effectively and, if he agrees, it is useful for his progress to be monitored by others who are in frequent personal contact with him such as the following:

Line management: The immediate supervisor can keep an eye on lateness and absence and other items in Checklist 2.

Personnel officers: Personnel officers can monitor absences and they are in a position to evaluate medical certificates and, if there is no improvement, to refer the problem drinker to the occupational physician.

Occupational nurse: The occupational nurse is in a good position to detect problem drinkers at work, particularly when it comes to accidents and requests for antacids.

Occupational physician: The occupational physician may receive reports from the personnel officers or line management. The evaluation of certificates started by the personnel section can be taken a stage further through an initial detailed examination and assessment of the employee. If the problem drinker decides to try to control his own drinking, further checkups (and offers of help) at agreed intervals can be arranged.

The above staff are in an excellent position to identify and monitor problem drinkers when it comes to absence from work or reduced work performance.

Of course, many items in Checklists 1 and 2 could constitute a breach of the employee/employer contract and could lead to the dismissal of the problem drinker in some cases. The alternative to dismissal is to offer the problem drinker understanding and, if necessary, the opportunity for appropriate treatment.

This will all cost the company more money in addition to the output which has already been lost by the problem drinker, and key employees will be tied up in helping him and in monitoring his recovery. Is it worth it? The next section looks at the financial implications of having a problem drinker on the payroll and argues that an Employment Alcohol Policy, which offers help to a firm's problem drinkers, would be financially worthwhile in many cases.

Employment Alcohol Policy

- **Is it worth it?**
The problem drinker in a firm can cost an employer a substantial amount of money. Common examples are:

Accidents at work involving personal injury to the problem drinker or a workmate.

Third party claims arising from faulty workmanship.

Third party claims arising from accidents involving heavy plant, HGVs or PSVs.

Expensive plant standing idle.

Other financial implications for any large firm can be calculated roughly. Adapting the work of Carl Schramm, it is possible to set out a cost analysis from two assumptions which are based on a wide variety of data.

Assumption 1
An average of 4% of the workforce are problem drinkers. The actual percentage varies from company to company. If the workforce was primarily women under 25, for example, the percentage would probably be low. If it consisted of men between 35 and 45 in heavy industry, the percentage may be high.

Assumption 2
Employees with a drink problem are 30–40% less productive on average than other workers. This figure takes into account absence, sickness, lowered efficiency and poor work relationships.

The resulting cost analysis gives a rough estimate of the potential cost of problem drinking in a workforce of 1,000 employees. It represents an attempt to put a figure on the potential cost of problem drinking.

Cost analysis table		
Total employees on payroll		1,000
Number of problem drinkers –		
Assumption 1	1,000 × 4%	=40
Average annual wage of each worker		£7,500
Wages paid to problem drinkers –		
Assumption 1	£7,500 × 40	=£300,000
Annual costs of reduced productivity –		
Assumption 2	£300,000 × 35%	**=£105,000**

The total cost of reduced productivity because of problem drinkers of £105,000 a year does not take into account accidents or damaged plant. If we assume that there will be a 30% reduction in the number of employees with a drink problem (in the example, from 40 to 28) when an Employment Alcohol Policy has been adopted, the savings would amount to £31,500 (30% of £105,000) which would be considerably more than the cost of setting up and administering the Employment Alcohol Policy.

- **Setting up your own Employment Alcohol Policy**
  Setting up an alcohol policy has three objectives:

  Awareness of what alcohol is and the effect it has
  (see Chapter 2).
  Early identification of drink problems
  (see Checklists 1, 2 and 3 in this chapter).
  Appropriate treatment for problem drinkers (see Chapter 8).

Before you can establish an Employment Alcohol Policy within an organisation there are certain conditions which you should try to meet. These ensure that everybody in a firm knows what is happening and why.

Conditions of an Alcohol Employment Policy

Members of the Board and senior managers must accept that problem drinking may affect within the firm and they need to agree that an Alcohol Employment Policy should become part of company procedures.

The personnel and welfare departments, together with occupational medical staff, need to establish clear procedures for identifying problem drinkers and for monitoring their progress.

The company needs to consider employing a specialist agency which is able to advise on alcohol problems and on the various methods of treatment.

The policy should be set up with the full cooperation of the appropriate unions.

The organisation and employees need to recognise how serious the problem is. However, it must be made quite clear that setting up the policy is not a 'witch hunt' but an attempt to

● improve the productivity and efficiency of the organisation;

● improve the health, welfare and social conditions of the staff.

Any Employment Alcohol Policy needs to be tailored to the needs of the organisation. Most of the initiative in Great Britain has come from the brewing industry. Brewing is a high risk occupation and so the industry has a potentially large number of problem drinkers, though it is not clear how many employees become problem drinkers because they work in the industry and how many people look for work in the industry because they already have a drink problem. This could mean that an automatic screening of recruits for a drink problem becomes part of a particular firm's Employment Alcohol Policy in order to prevent high risk drinkers being recruited.

Whether or not the Employment Alcohol Policy drawn up for your firm allows for the routine screening of would-be employees, it should always include the three objectives of **awareness**, **identification** and **treatment**.

Awareness
It is important to build an alcohol awareness theme into the Policy from the very beginning because experience has shown that it helps to prevent inappropriate drinking. Employees are not often aware of the potential consequences of drinking even fairly small amounts of alcohol – one or two pints of beer – during the working day.

One way of encouraging awareness is to display some appropriate eye-catching posters. One which is extremely effective shows an ambulance speeding out of the works' gates with the caption:

If you drink at lunchtime you may leave work a little earlier than you expected.

Unfortunately, posters quickly become dog-eared and other people pin new notices over them. This means that you need to keep an eye on the noticeboards and to change posters regularly to keep the topic fresh in people's minds. Another way to encourage awareness is to use a fact pack. Several large employers in Great Britain have developed folders of material on alcohol which are given out to each employee. The advantage of fact packs is that they can be updated by handing out new sheets when needed. Employers can design their own packs with the help of one of the specialist alcohol agencies (see Appendix 1). Topics to include are:

How alcohol is produced
How alcohol affects the body
Alcohol and the family
Warning signs of a drink problem
How to get help for an alcohol related problem
A copy of the Employment Alcohol Policy (see page 85)

The best approach is probably to use bright, well designed posters and folders together. Some employers have also found that seminars and discussion groups organised by unions and management are an effective way of increasing their workforce's awareness of alcohol.

Identification
Checklists on how to identify drink problems at work are on pages 80 and 81.

If any Employment Alcohol Policy is to work effectively, it will be necessary to make sure that appropriate staff are properly trained. Those who will be responsible for detecting problem drinking and for offering help will need to be well-informed so that anyone with a problem can feel confident in approaching them.

Many of the staff involved in implementing the Employment Alcohol Policy will already have some of the skills needed because they are the skills of man management. They will, nevertheless, need to know how to apply their skills to alcohol related problems and this can only be achieved through training by a specialist alcohol agency (see Appendix 1). The Alcohol Education Centre has developed a table which is adapted here. It shows nine different sections of company staff who need special training. The training is split into two parts, **information** and **skills**.

Members of the company who need training	See **information** section numbers	See **skills** section numbers
Company Board	1,2	-
Senior Management	1,2	4,5
All employees	1	-
Groups at special risk of developing a drink problem	1	5
Supervisors/line managers	1	1,4
Personnel department	1,5	2,4
Occupational health staff	1,3,4	2,3
Safety officers	1,5	4,5
Welfare officers	1	3,5
Union officials	1,2	1,4

Figure 9: Members of the company who need training

Information: Staff need to have accurate and objective information about alcohol generally and particularly about its effects on work.

These five points relate to the numbers shown in the **Information** column of Figure 9.

1   *Basic understanding:* Once a person has a basic understanding of alcohol and alcoholism, he needs to be able to relate it to his own drinking habits and to those of his colleagues. He also needs to appreciate exactly what the company Employment Alcohol Policy means and to know what procedures have been agreed for dealing with drink problems.

2   *Alcohol at work:* The aim here is to have a broad knowledge of research into the problems of excessive drinking in employment contexts and to be able to relate the findings of this research to the ways in which an Employment Alcohol Policy is developed.

3   *Alcoholism:* It is necessary to have an accurate and up-to-date knowledge of the nature, cause and effects of alcoholism.

4   *Sources of treatment:* It is important to be aware of all the local and national agencies which offer help to problem drinkers and to know their strengths and weaknesses so that a problem drinker can be referred to the most appropriate one. It is also useful to maintain good relationships with all these agencies (see Appendix 1).

5   *Alcohol consumption and work performance:* Someone, such as the safety officer, will need to know about research findings which show how alcohol consumption is related to performance so that he can apply his knowledge to specific work contexts.

Skills: Some staff will need training in the skills they need to carry out the Employment Alcohol Policy and to deal with what are likely to be sensitive problems. There are five types of skills which may be needed.

These five points relate to the numbers shown in the **Skills** column of Figure 9.

1   *Identify:* It is vital to be able to identify signs which show that someone may have an alcohol problem (see Checklists in this chapter).

2   *Assess:* The need here is to be able to assess individual cases when a possible alcohol problem has been detected. The

assessment should include a consideration of which form of treatment (inside or outside the firm) would probably be the most appropriate if drinking is confirmed as a problem. In some cases, disciplinary procedures may be appropriate.

3   *Help:* Either occupational health staff or welfare officers should be able to offer appropriate help, such as counselling, to employees who have been identified as problem drinkers. They may be able to offer counselling themselves or they may need to offer outside help through an efficient and confidential referral system.

4   *Monitor:* There are a number of staff who should be able to monitor the improvement of people who have returned to work after treatment (or who continue at work while being treated). They need to be sensitive enough to be able to notice the reappearance of the problem.

5   *Minimise the likelihood of a drink problem:* Any Employment Alcohol Policy should try to minimise the risk of both short and long-term drinking problems at work. There should be a group of people responsible for minimising the risk of a drink problem either by education or, if necessary, by controlling the availability of alcohol.

Treatment
In the context of an Employment Alcohol Policy, treatment means any form of intervention which can relieve a drink problem. Medical treatment may be needed if the problem is serious but treatment can often mean no more than a programme of specialised counselling.

It is probably best if a firm which is thinking about developing an Employment Alcohol Policy contacts the specialist alcohol agencies in its area (see Appendix 1) in order to work out a system of intervention which can be put into action as soon as a problem drinker is identified. In the USA, some large companies and the armed forces actually employ 'alcohol counsellors' who often have their offices in the personnel department.

This system has the advantages of inbuilt monitoring for problem drinkers who have been treated and of being available in the workplace itself. However, experience suggests that some people prefer the impartial anonymity of a third party such as a counsellor from the local Council on Alcoholism.

- *The basic components of an Employment Alcohol Policy*
Although no two Employment Alcohol Policies are exactly alike because each company has its own priorities, there are some elements which are common to the majority of policies which have been established up to now:

The employer recognises that the problem drinker is someone who needs treatment and that the difficulty should be dealt with in the same way as any other health problem.

When someone with a drinking problem is identified, he should be encouraged to seek help and treatment on the understanding that:

- He will be regarded as being on sick leave if he has to be admitted to hospital. This means that he is entitled to normal rights and privileges.

- If he does not have to be given sick leave, he should be given the necessary time off to keep appointments with an alcohol counsellor.

- His position with the company is secure and his job within the company will only be changed with his agreement.

- If the employee relapses, consideration will be given to further treatment.

- Disciplinary action will be suspended unless the problem drinker refuses advice and guidance and/or continues to drink in a way which affects his work.

- The policy applies to all employees including senior management.

- *A written policy or an informal policy?*
Recent experience indicates that a written policy is more useful for all concerned. The advantages of a written policy are that it is a clear statement of company procedure in dealing with alcohol in the workplace and that a copy of the policy can be included in a fact pack which is distributed to all employees. A further advantage is that negotiations and discussions

which take place before the policy is implemented should ensure that it is acceptable to both management and employees.

The disadvantage of an unwritten or informal policy is that it can often lead to discrepancies and to some employees being treated differently to others. Informal agreements also have a habit of disappearing when management changes take place.

- **The legal context**
  The Health and Safety at Work Act 1974 makes it clear that an employer has a duty to, 'ensure, so far as is reasonably practicable, the health, safety and welfare at work of all his employees'. The Act specifies the, 'provision of information, instruction and training to ensure health and safety'. This can provide a legal framework for an Employment Alcohol Policy.

  Up to now, an emphasis has been laid on the responsibility of the employer but the employee also has a duty under the Act which is to, 'take reasonable care for the health and safety of himself and of other persons who may be affected by his acts or omissions at work'.

- **Results**
  Studies in the USA, where many firms have adopted Employment Alcohol Policies, indicate that successful rehabilitation is as high as 50–70%. The New York Transit Authority, which employs 34,000 people, has published figures which show that whilst it cost $325,000 over five years to operate an Employment Alcohol Policy, the saving in sick pay alone amounted to $1.5m.

  There are so few Employment Alcohol Policies in operation in Great Britain at present that no statistically significant results have been obtained. However, some of those firms which do operate such a policy have provided some extremely interesting individual success stories. Take the case of Fred who was a maintainance fitter working in the textile industry. He had been employed by the same company for 15 years, he was highly experienced and would be hard to replace.

Fred

Fred, a married man aged 38, was a heavy social drinker whose drinking had begun to affect his work. He worked on shifts and had been sent home when he had turned up for work smelling of drink on several occasions. The event which led to him being identified as

*a problem drinker was when he arrived at work intoxicated but had
not been noticed by management. He started to re-assemble a
machine which would normally have taken him a couple of hours.
When the machine operator asked him why he was taking so long
he became aggressive and was later found to be intoxicated.*

*He was referred to the local Council on Alcoholism which
arranged to see him at weekly intervals. Fred was also receiving
treatment from his own doctor. Contact was maintained for three
months during which time Fred did not drink at all. His work
performance was not affected by drinking when he started to drink
again, after six months, in a pattern negotiated with his
counsellor. No work problems have arisen during a two year period
and Fred continues to see his counsellor at monthly intervals or
when he feels in danger of drinking in a way which is likely to
affect his work.*

The outcome in Fred's case was good. He was identified,
assessed and appropriate treatment and follow up were
arranged. However, success is not always so easy to achieve.

John
*John was a 49–year-old single man who worked as a chemical
process supervisor. He was in charge of six process workers, was
very experienced and had been employed by the firm for 25 years.
Unlike Fred, John never arrived at work smelling of drink. In fact,
he never went to work if he had been drinking. His absences were
tolerated because he was a long serving employee but over a three
year period his absences had resulted in a total of 48 weeks off
work. He was referred to an alcohol counselling service which, in
turn, referred him to an Alcohol Treatment Unit, where he was an
in-patient for eight weeks.*

*On discharge he returned to work and did well for three months.
Then he began to go absent from work again and refused further
treatment. John was too young to be retired on the grounds of ill
health but he was dismissed and was paid his pension
contributions. After spending all this money he turned up on the
doorstep of the Alcohol Treatment Unit. He was re-admitted, but
only for a short period of 'drying out'. When he was discharged, he
went for six weeks without drinking but could not find a job.*

*He eventually returned to his former employer who agreed to
accept him back as an ordinary process worker on probation with
the condition that, if he was absent because of his drinking, he
would be immediately dismissed and not reconsidered. He kept to*

*his 'contract' and after 12 months he was given back his old job as
a supervisor when the person who had originally replaced him
moved on.*

In John's case, the outcome was not successful immediately. However, treatment provided a long-term benefit for John himself and for his employer who did not have to provide training for a new supervisor.

There are major potential benefits not only for employers but also for the community when a greater effort is made to identify problem drinkers at work. Admittedly, the impact of drinking on employment varies and some companies are likely to be more affected than others. However, because drinking problems are present in nearly all social groups, it is wise to be alert. A written Employment Alcohol Policy is advisable in all high risk occupational groups.

The brewing industry has led the field in adopting policies. It is up to other industries to follow its lead and to feel the benefit of better productivity, of a reduced number of accidents at work and, if the American experience is shared, of large financial savings.

5 Alcohol and crime

Introduction

It seems a fair estimate that drink is involved in about 60% of the crime committed by the habitual criminals who form a large part of the prison population. In 1980, the Parole Board expressed concern about the high number of prisoners serving terms of 18 months or more whose crimes had often been committed because of their drinking. As for crimes of violence, research in France has indicated that 60% of violent offences are committed by 'alcoholics' and in England and Wales it is likely that over 50% of offences of a violent nature, particularly those which occur late at night, are committed near public houses by people who have been drinking. In 1970, the Council of Europe estimated that 60% of child cruelty comes from a background of problem drinking. Problem drinking is also associated with many cases of assault on wives (and husbands!).

Drinking is often involved in a wide variety of other crimes from road traffic offences, where an offender has drunk 'over the limit' to burglary, where an offender has had a few drinks to give himself courage. There is also the whole range of drunkenness offences.

Although there is little doubt that a connection between crime and drinking exists, it is notoriously difficult to discover those offenders whose drinking constitutes a real problem. The checklists in Chapters 2 and 3 of this book may help, and factors such as environment, home situation, family, work prospects, financial status and general health all need to be taken into account.

The people who are most likely to notice that an offender has a drink problem are those who come into contact with him during the judicial process such as:

Police officers
Solicitors
Officers of the court
Probation officers
Social workers
Prison staff

All these people have a role to play in the detection of a problem drinker who is probably at a critical phase in his drinking career and will possibly agree to accept some form of help or treatment. They are in a position to make observations which, correctly interpreted, may lead to advice and assistance for the problem drinking offender. A list of agencies who provide specialised help can be found in Appendix 1.

What offences?

Crimes which are committed as a consequence of drinking fall into two categories, **primary** and **secondary** offences.

- *Primary offences*
These are offences where drinking or obtaining drink was a central feature of the crime and had a direct bearing on the offence committed.

Drunkenness
Simple public drunkenness, being drunk and disorderly or being drunk and incapable are offences. Arguments have raged for over a hundred years about how to treat people found guilty of drunkenness.

The following exchange could well have taken place in a Parliamentary Select Committee in 1981 when a Prison Governor was asked by the Chairman of the Committee, 'In your opinion, what is the effect of the existing method of punishing the drunken offender by imposing short terms of imprisonment?'. The Governor replied, 'I think it is quite useless and that it does more harm than good.'

That exchange, in fact, took place in 1872 and the Committee recommended that drunken offenders be taken to 'inebriate homes'. A hundred years later, in 1972, the Criminal Justice Act laid down procedures for the provision of Detoxification Centres where habitual drunken offenders could be sent for 'drying out'. The first one, which was community-based, was opened in Leeds in 1976, and the second, which was a hospital-based Detoxification Unit, was opened in Manchester in the following year.

The failure to establish any more centres despite the success demonstrated in Leeds and Manchester in terms of human, financial and time savings, means that a great army of police, magistrates, probation officers, social workers and prison officers continue to have a role to play in the treatment of people who get drunk in public and remain, until decriminalisation is achieved, primary offenders.

Staff in Probation Duty Offices, Social Services Offices and hospital Accident and Emergency Departments often have to deal with belligerent, demanding and intoxicated visitors. In cases like this it is useless to try and talk to them. What can be done is to encourage a *contract* to see them the following day or after the weekend, before they get drunk again. It is important to stress that there is no reason to feel guilty because you cannot do anything, provided that someone who is drunk is not allowed to leave when he is likely to be a danger to himself or to other people. If he is a danger, the police should be called.

Road traffic accidents
Driving a motor vehicle with a blood alcohol level greater than 80 mg% (see page 281) is an offence. It is estimated that, in a large number of fatal accidents, the driver's blood alcohol level is over the prescribed limit. In fact, a blood alcohol level in excess of 50 mg% makes the possibility of an accident much greater because judgment can be impaired and inhibitions decreased. It is when inhibitions diminish that a driver feels more confident than usual and is more likely to take risks, with sometimes fatal results.

Many people do not know how much alcohol there is in various drinks and even more do not know how alcohol is treated by the body. There is no such thing as a 'safe limit' once you have begun drinking, although people who drink less than 50 grams of alcohol may remain under the 80 mg% permitted limits. Nevertheless, the risk of having an accident is greater than if they had not drunk any alcohol.

50 grams of alcohol are contained in:
Five half pints of ordinary beer
Five pub measures of spirits
Five ordinary glasses of wine
Five small glasses of port, sherry or vermouth
(drunk over a period of two hours)

There is also the possibility that alcohol may still be in the bloodstream from a previous drinking session (see Figure 4 on page 35).

The Blennerhassett Report in 1976 made recommendations about drinking and driving which have not yet been fully implemented. A considerable amount of the report looked at the implications of problem drinking. The report believed that many people who drank regularly and heavily were also drivers and that they presented a more serious threat to road safety than other drivers who drank less regularly and more moderately. Identifying the so-called high risk offender is difficult but the Blennerhassett Report concluded that he was someone who was convicted twice within 10 years on a charge of drunken driving. Implicit in the report was that a first offence which involved a blood alcohol level over 200 mg% also pointed to a high risk, which made it possible to identify a potential problem drinker without having to wait for a second offence and perhaps a fatal accident.

It does not follow that everyone who is convicted of drunken driving is a problem drinker. Someone who is normally a moderate drinker may have driven over the limit on an isolated occasion, say after a birthday party. But, despite the possibility of treating someone for a non-existent drink problem, screening everyone who is convicted of drinking and driving may well lead to better road safety. It may also help to identify more 'alcoholics' who are in the early stages of a drink problem, and an appropriate intervention may well lead to benefits for the driver's family and his employer as well as for himself.

Even though recommendations in the Blennerhassett Report have not been implemented, it should still be possible for the magistrates in any area, in conjunction with the Justices' Clerks' Department and with the help of the local Consultant on Alcoholism or the local Council on Alcoholism, to devise a method of intervention. Perhaps an information sheet could be given to an offender after the court case was over (see Figure 10).

There is no reason why people should not also be referred by their solicitors to Alcohol Advice Centres or any other specialist alcohol agency (see Appendix 1).

Offences of violence
Weekend and Monday courts are often full of the casualties of Friday, Saturday and Sunday night entertainment in cities and towns. Before they reach court, many of these people will also have passed through the local Accident and Emergency

Drinking and driving

People who are convicted of drinking and driving have either been foolish, thinking they would get away with it, or they have been unaware of the effects of alcohol and have not realised they were driving 'over the limit'.

Some drinking drivers also have a serious drink problem.

Whichever kind of drinking driver you are, you may like more information about how drink can affect you, or you may like to talk to someone about your drinking habits. Drinking and driving can be very costly: *don't risk it again*.

Please contact:
Fordtown Council on Alcoholism
(confidential information and advice service)
Tel: Fordtown 12345

Figure 10: Drinking and driving information sheet

Department to have their battle scars treated. Common features of many of the skirmishes in which these people have received their injuries are that they will have taken place near public houses and that they will have been started by people who have lost control over their tempers because they have had too much to drink.

Football matches are often attended by people who are passionate supporters of their team and work up a hate for the opposition supporters which is fuelled by large quantities of drink. This hate often turns into street violence after the match has ended. Other sporting events also have their share of problems caused by excessive drinking.

At home as well, people can lose control over their drinking because of a 'few too many'. Over half of violent attacks on wives are committed either after or during a drinking session by husbands who drink heavily. Studies which have examined the relationship between drinking and murder have shown that the killer was intoxicated in around 50% of the cases.

However, in some cases, alcohol may have been used solely to give the offender the courage to commit the crime.

Sexual offences are often committed by people who would not have done so if their behaviour had not been affected by alcohol. Although drinking may not be the immediate cause of the offence, it may well be part of a much wider problem.

Offences of dishonesty
Drinking is a costly activity and many 'alcoholics' find themselves having to steal alcohol. The offender may be intoxicated or in a state of withdrawal (see page 36).

Single homeless 'alcoholics' are often pressured into stealing by members of the 'drinking gang' (see Chapter 6) and their most common targets are small shops and off-licences where a theft is likely to go unnoticed because of diversionary tactics and a lack of sophisticated anti-theft systems. Supermarkets in large towns and cities are also favourite targets for the habitual drunken offenders. These people are usually dependent upon alcohol and, once they have spent all their money on drink, their dependence means that they have to obtain further supplies by any means possible. They never stop to think about the consequences of what they are doing.

Although it is usually difficult to involve this type of offender in a treatment programme, he will often agree to some form of intervention when he appears before the court. In this case, his solicitor can be in an ideal position to obtain a report from the probation service, a consultant psychiatrist, a local Council on Alcoholism or a local single homeless project.

An effective way of dealing with this type of offender is for the court to impose a deferred sentence. This type of sentence can give the offender an incentive and a real opportunity to modify the drinking pattern which has led to the offence, or to cut out drinking altogether. There have been some success stories such as Barry who was referred to an Alcohol Advice Centre by his solicitor. He had stolen three shirts from a city centre store.

Barry
Now 40, Barry left school at the age of 15 and had several manual jobs before being called up for National Service. Later, he decided to sign on as a regular soldier. He started to drink heavily in the army and was discharged on medical grounds after six years because he had developed an ulcer.

He had many jobs over a 10 year period and, after his parents died, he drifted into a very unsettled life, finding work in hotels. He was fined for numerous offences of drunkenness and served several short prison sentences for petty theft and non-payment of fines. Three weeks after he was discharged from his last prison sentence he took to 'sleeping rough'. He had spent all his money on drink and had stolen some shirts to sell and so enable him to buy more drink.

Barry's offences were more of a nuisance than a danger to society and the court was asked to defer sentence while treatment was offered for his drinking. He was in poor physical and emotional shape and was completely socially isolated. Barry was admitted to an Alcohol Treatment Unit where he spent six weeks. When he left hospital he was offered a place in an aftercare house. He stopped drinking completely and settled into the house with people whose company he enjoyed. When he appeared before court at the end of the deferment, he was conditionally discharged. He soon found a part-time job and remained living in the house.

Barry's case shows what can be achieved when a drink problem is detected and appropriate treatment offered, even when the harmful drinking goes back over many years. There is a high risk that Barry will return to heavy drinking at some point but the benefits of his treatment will still be quite considerable. The skills which people like Barry learn during the 'dry' period often enable them to function much better despite going back to drinking. They acquire some social skills (see page 184) and learn how drink affects them. Because they know about the effect of drink, it means that they often make fewer appearances in the courts. They also know what facilities are available to help them and they do not need to wait to be referred again.

Sentencing which is deferred for about three months seems to be most appropriate for cases such as Barry's since this is the period of treatment which has been seen to offer most in terms of a significant early improvement in problem drinking. As for eventual sentencing, a probation order (see page 108) from the court can be useful but a conditional discharge (see page 107) is often more appropriate because an offender will already have completed the initial phase of a treatment programme by this stage. A conditional discharge is not a 'let off' because any further offence would result in a more serious penalty.

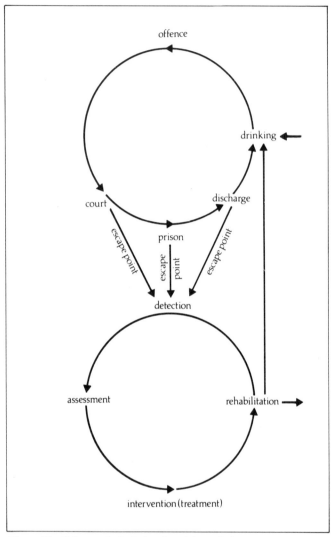

Figure 11: Crime and alcohol – the vicious circle

The offender's incentive is not only an improvement in health, accommodation and social status but also an opportunity to escape from the vicious circle shown in Figure 11.

- **Secondary offences**

  In primary offences there is a direct link between alcohol and the offence which is committed. The link between alcohol and secondary offences is much more difficult to establish. Secondary offences are often committed by people who are just beginning to develop a drink problem. There are two categories of secondary offences:

  - Offences which are committed by the drinker himself.
  - Offences which are committed by a member of the drinker's family.

  Several types of offence can fall into these categories, such as theft, shoplifting, pilfering, fraud, robbery and mugging. The link between these offences and problem drinking may not be immediately apparent but, in almost every case, the connection will turn out to be financial hardship caused by problem drinking. You need money to buy alcohol and if the crime itself does not produce money, it can produce goods which can then be turned into ready cash. In other cases, the motive for the offence, particularly when a member of the drinker's family is involved, may have been to find the money to pay bills or to provide basic necessities such as food and clothing, when all the usual income has been spent on alcohol.

  People who deal with these types of case and find it hard to understand the reasons for a crime can use the Checklists in Chapters 2 and 3, as well as the methods of assessment which are outlined in Chapter 7, to discover whether an offender has a drink problem or whether someone in his family may be a problem drinker.

  The person asked to prepare a report on the offender is often best placed to unearth a drink problem. The court or the defence will often ask for a report on the offender's background and circumstances. The report enables the court to make a more informed decision about sentencing. Whoever is asked to write the report should always try to find out about the part which drinking – especially heavy drinking – plays in the offender's life and in the lives of other members of his family. Four important questions which should be kept in mind are shown in this checklist.

Drinking and secondary offences – Checklist

How much does the person drink? (Always try to check with other members of the family that this is accurate.)

If the person drinks heavily, how long has this been going on?

How does the cost of drinking compare to income?

What effects does drink seem to have on behaviour?

The best way to show how this checklist can work in practice is by means of three very different case studies.

Ken
Ken was a 45-year-old man who had been divorced and had remarried. He had served several prison sentences for petty offences, and on this occasion he appeared before the court for the theft of a colour television set which he had rented. Past social enquiry reports had described family problems, long periods of unemployment and poverty, and had even mentioned that he had been discharged from the army for assaulting an officer. However, no enquiries had ever been made about Ken's drinking.

At the time that he committed the TV offence, his expectant wife had left him, he had lost his job and there were rent arrears. He had sold the TV to pay off his debts but, on his way home, he had called into the local pub for a quick one, had met friends who had been helping him out for the past two weeks and had spent most of the money that he received from the sale of the TV on repaying them and on buying drinks.

Ken never considered that he had a drink problem and previous statutory supervision, intended to deal with his family problems by helping him to find work and by paying off his debts, had always failed because his drinking had never been dealt with.

When the checklist is applied to Ken's case, it shows that:

- He drinks roughly 70 pints of beer a week.

- He has been drinking for many years and he has lost jobs because of his drinking.

- Drink costs Ken over half of his income.

- He has stolen a TV and spent part of the proceeds on drink.

Dawn
Dawn was a 33-year-old married woman who appeared before the

court on a shoplifting charge, her first offence. She had gone into a shop and bought a few items. However, she had also dropped four tins of meat into her shopping bag on the way round. The Magistrates gave her a conditional discharge and warned her about what would happen if she was caught shoplifting again.

A probation officer in court felt uneasy about the whole thing and followed her out of court. After a short chat, Dawn agreed to telephone the probation officer to make an appointment to see her again. The probation officer eventually discovered that Dawn's husband left her very short of money and with nothing in the house. Dawn was frightened of asking for more money because her requests were always met with an aggressive response – and even less money!

When the checklist is applied to Dawn's case, it shows that:

- Dawn's husband drinks 8 pints of beer a day.

- He has been drinking heavily for about two years.

- His drinking absorbs a large proportion of the family income.

- He becomes aggressive towards his family.

It is important that Dawn is seen as someone with a problem herself – being married to a heavy drinker. She needs help to develop a way of dealing with her problem which does not involve crime. It would also be appropriate to try, though probably without success in this case, to get her husband to accept some form of treatment. Eventually, some form of marital therapy might be possible.

Ronnie
Ronnie was a 13-year-old only child who had a very poor school attendance record. Attempts by teachers, social workers and education welfare officers to encourage him to go to school more often failed. Even on days he went to school, he would leave at lunchtime. He started to steal money which led to him being brought before the juvenile court. Ronnie's father often worked away from home and his mother was left on her own to cope with Ronnie. Ronnie had begun to worry about her because he had found her lying asleep, with an empty bottle at her side, when he came home. Naturally, Ronnie was sensitive about this and could not speak to anyone about it.

Ronnie's is a much more complex case than the other two, in that it is very unlikely that it would ever be considered that a drinking problem in his family was the cause of the trouble.

However, applying the checklist to Ronnie's mother shows that:

- She drinks almost half a bottle of gin a day.

- She has been drinking heavily for some six months.

- Her drinking costs about a third of her housekeeping money.

- She feels unable to manage the household, she is not able to look after Ronnie properly and her behaviour worries Ronnie.

The effect of this family problem was quite damaging on Ronnie and a supervision order may well be the outcome in his case. However, the main feature of the supervision order may be appropriate treatment for the mother's drink problem in addition to therapy sessions for the whole family.

The specialist court report on the known problem drinker

When someone who has been identified as a problem drinker comes before the court, it may often be appropriate for some specialist information from a psychiatrist or alcohol counsellor to be supplied to the Judge or Magistrate to enable sentence to be passed.

It is useful to know what goes into a court report, whether or not you are ever called upon to write one. There are four important sections:

- **Background**
  Cultural and religious background
  Present social environment and relationships
  Relationships with family members
  Relevant information about childhood
  Education
  Employment and armed service history
  Current financial circumstances and commitments
  Medical and psychiatric history

- *Drinking and the offence*
  The effect of problem drinking on the person and his family (including financial hardship)
  The impact of drinking on present and previous offences
  Response to previous treatment

- *Intervention and treatment*
  The court wants to know what kind of alternative to custody can be considered appropriate. This will often have been the most difficult part of the report to write and it is important that it should be both objective and realistic if it is to help guide the court into passing a sentence which will allow some form of intervention and treatment. Some comment on how successful a particular sentence may be can also be included. (The benefits of deferred sentences have already been referred to on page 100.)

- *Conclusions and recommendations*
  The conclusions should say why intervention is being recommended and it is important that they should say if treatment is not likely to be effective. This may be the case if all previous attempts at treatment have failed. Whether the report's recommendations are accepted is up to the court.

Commonly used sentences

- *Absolute/conditional discharge*
  This sentence is used for offences which are not serious or where there is no previous criminal record. An absolute discharge can be given when a person is bailed for a drunkenness offence and responds to treatment for his problem drinking before his court appearance.

- *Fine*
  This sentence often causes problems, particularly for the single, homeless offender who has little money. The risk is that non-payment of the fine often results in imprisonment.

- *Deferred sentence*
  Postponing the sentence for a fixed period (see page 100).

- **Probation order**

  This means that an offender is supervised for a fixed period of time. Usually this is between six months and three years. A probation order can be particularly helpful when it seems that the problem drinker will need support for more than three months. It is also a useful sentence when the family and the problem drinker need to find their feet again.

- **Community service order (CSO)**

  As a general rule, community service officers are reluctant to take on problem drinkers unless they have shown signs of responding to treatment. A CSO can often help an 'alcoholic' whose drink problem is improving to regain self respect and confidence.

- **Binding over**

  Being bound over in a certain sum is often the sentence passed on the undetected problem drinker who has 'offended against the public order'. He has to be 'of good behaviour' for a specified length of time or he forfeits the money.

- **Suspended and prison sentences**

  Many problem drinkers find their way into the 'vicious circle' shown on page 102 (Figure 11) when they are given prison sentences, as many of them are. However, the sentence may be suspended for a period of time (usually two years) and, if no more offences are committed, the slate is wiped clean. Unfortunately, experience shows that a high percentage of 'alcoholics' whose drinking problem goes undetected do re-offend, often with monotonous regularity.

Problem drinking offenders in prison

Current attitudes to sentencing seem to indicate that imprisonment is only used when:

The crime is a serious offence.

There is a pattern of similar offences and other sentences have failed.

There is no realistic alternative.

Some 'alcoholics' may be sent to prison on a number of occasions without their drink problem being detected. This could well be because prisons are so overcrowded and prison staff so occupied that there is no chance of identifying a prisoner with a drink problem, let alone assessing the extent of his problem and getting him to agree to treatment. In addition, unless withdrawal symptoms are acute enough to warrant medical attention, a prisoner may well 'dry out' during the course of a sentence because no alcohol is available in prison. However, some appropriate interventions can be made by:

- **Prison medical staff**
  The medical staff in a prison are able to review prisoners' health and diagnose alcohol related disorders and withdrawal symptoms (see Chapter 2). If this information is fed to the prison probation officer and, in turn, to the home aftercare probation officer, it may be possible to organise appropriate treatment once a prisoner is released.

- **Prison psychological staff**
  Many problem drinking offenders have psychological difficulties which may be dealt with by means of group therapy, social skills training and behaviour modification (see Chapters 9 and 10). If some alcohol education is included in these programmes, it may help the prisoner to have a better chance of breaking out of the vicious circle detailed on page 102 (Figure 11).

- **Prison officers**
  Officers are in day to day contact with groups of prisoners. They are able to notice changes and to discuss problems with prisoners. If they suspect that a problem involves drinking, they should be in a position to alert appropriate prison staff such as the medical or psychological staff or the prison probation officer.

- **Prison probation officers**
  Prison probation officers usually see the sentenced men when they arrive at a prison and they receive a copy of the prisoner's social enquiry report, which is a report on the prisoner prepared by the probation service before he is sentenced. Liaison between prison probation officers and the home probation

officer who is in contact with the family can help the prisoner with a drink problem and his family to start thinking about ways of dealing with the problem while he is serving his sentence. Prison probation officers can also contact a specialist alcohol agency (see Appendix 1) which can offer help to the prisoner as soon as he is discharged.

- *Alcoholics Anonymous (see page 149)*
Some prisons allow a member of Alcoholics Anonymous to attend the prison and to hold weekly meetings. AA groups are a useful way of getting a prisoner to think about how drinking has contributed to his problems. He may continue to attend local meetings of Alcoholics Anonymous after he is discharged.

It has already been pointed out that some drink problems can 'disappear' simply because there is no temptation or opportunity to drink in prison. This means that interventions which may have been spectacularly successful in prison are subject to all sorts of pressures when a prisoner is discharged. There is the urge to have a 'celebration' drink and many aftercare probation officers who are prepared to offer support find that the discharged man has spent all of his discharge grant on getting drunk. In an attempt to end this frustration, some prisoners are now met at the prison gates!

When a problem drinking offender appears before the court he may well be at a stage where his problem can be identified. It is important that the problem should be identified and that some form of intervention should take place at this stage so that a case may be made for appropriate sentencing. Suitable intervention can also mean that the offender does not enter the vicious circle of offence and punishment which is shown on page 102 (Figure 11). Although treatment will not be successful in every case, even a few successes will mean benefits for society in terms of fewer crimes and less demand being made on the health and social services.

6 Down and out on skid row

Introduction

For the man or woman who has nowhere to live, whose income is limited or non-existent and who regularly abuses alcohol, life is full of very special problems. The first is to know where the next drink is coming from, the second is to be able to cope with a variety of illnesses brought on by drinking and the third, in a long list, is to manage to survive without means. It is important that anyone who chooses to work with these people, who make up about 5% of the total 'alcoholic' population of Great Britain, should be aware of their particular problems.

Skid row is the collective term which originated in the USA and is most often used now to describe single, homeless and often 'alcoholic' people. The members of skid row, homeless for a variety of reasons, are forced to rub along with each other in using the facilities provided for homeless people such as day shelters, common lodging houses and government resettlement units. Together, they learn how to survive, they develop common attitudes to outside society, they find acceptance and comradeship, and they discover an identity for themselves.

Any social worker or voluntary worker who tries to help a homeless 'alcoholic' will find himself facing not just the problems associated with alcohol abuse but also the hardened attitudes developed on skid row. These attitudes will act as a barrier to successful rehabilitation and as much time may have to be devoted to breaking them down as to the drink problem itself.

Identifying someone from skid row

The alienation, suspicion and shame associated with skid row often lead a single homeless 'alcoholic' to try to deceive anyone who tries to probe too deeply. However, when you are trying to find out about someone's background as a part of assessing how serious his drink problem is and how it should be treated (see Chapters 7 and 8) there are some clues which show whether or not he might be from skid row.

- **Homelessness**

  You should try to find out whether or not the person is homeless at the moment or has been homeless in the past and, if so, how often. How does he feel about not having a home to go to and is he frantic with worry as to what he is going to do? If he is aware that there is an alternative, whether it be sleeping rough (skippering), using day shelters or making use of some other accommodation you should suspect that he might belong to skid row.

- **Frequent moves and changes of occupation**

  Where does the person you are interviewing come from? How long has he been living locally? If he is local or has been living in the area for a long time, it may mean that he knows about day shelters, resettlement units and so on without being a member of skid row. It is possible he may still have family or friends he can contact, although relationships will probably be under some strain because of his drinking. However, it is worth remembering that, for some people, these local contacts will eventually break down and they will end up on skid row anyway. If someone has not lived in the area for very long and has moved around a lot this could be because he has worked in construction, seasonal agriculture, catering or other similar industries which are frequently the background for members of skid row (see page 78).

- **Living conditions**

  Where does the person normally live? This will probably be the most obvious sign of whether or not he is a member of skid row. Living in lodging houses or hostels usually indicates that someone is on skid row but even a respectable address can be deceptive because he may officially be staying with a friend, may be living in a lodging house that is not registered or may be living in a bed-sitter.

  Has the person ever occupied skid row type accommodation, and what were his impressions of it? Try to get some idea of whether or not this has influenced his present situation. If the person is homeless, he may be trying to hide this fact from shame, or from fear, because certain forms of welfare benefit depend upon his having an address.

  You need to be firm but reassuring when you ask for this information and must be prepared to say why you need it.

- *How does the person abuse alcohol?*
  Does the person drink in pubs and, if so, which ones? Are they the pubs which members of skid row prefer? If he drinks at home, does he drink alone or does he bring back a group of friends? It is worth bearing in mind that this group of friends may be a drinking gang, which is often formed on skid row. Does he drink in parks or other places outdoors where homeless people tend to congregate? Again, this will be an indication that he is closely involved in skid row.

  If there is a history of frequent arrests for public drunkenness, where has the person been arrested and in what circumstances? The habitual drunken offender is, by and large, the homeless or semi-homeless person who is less able to hide the signs of drunkenness than someone with a more established home.

- *What sort of alcohol does he drink?*
  Is he drinking spirits or cheap fortified wine? Has he progressed to drinking crude spirit (usually surgical spirits mixed with or 'boxed up with' other fluid), methylated spirits (both surgical and methylated spirits are known as 'Jake'), hair lacquer or similar cheap sources of alcohol? Has he ever done so in the past and if so, how did he feel about having reached this stage? Is his way of life any different now to what it was at that time? If he is drinking crude spirit at the moment, does he feel that his way of life is any different now from what it was four or five years ago?

Informal clues to identifying skid row 'alcoholics'

The person you are interviewing will always give subtle clues as to how he sees himself. You can often pick these clues up and use them to form a general impression of his attitude and situation. This is no less true for a homeless 'alcoholic' than for anyone else and he will give specific clues.

- *Use of slang*
  Like any other close-knit group skid row has a language all of its own which only people who belong know how to use properly. It indicates that the group is separate and different.

People use the language to show that they belong to the group and to show that they want to be seen as different. Skid row slang uses many expressions from the prison world because many homeless 'alcoholics' have passed through prison at some stage in their career.

It is useful for anyone working with skid row 'alcoholics' to know some of the terms himself so that he can recognise when someone wants to be identified as a member of skid row. Examples of skid row expressions are scattered throughout this chapter, but they will vary slightly from area to area.

- ## Glamorisation of skid row style

A sad fact of life for the homeless person who is living on his wits is that he will need skill, animal cunning and an instinct for survival second to none in order to exist on the streets. The organisation and sophistication of skid row that homeless 'alcoholics' sometimes talk about are nothing but an illusion. It is no more than an attempt to keep some personal pride and to justify what they are doing. Reality is often so depressing that their only escape lies in the rationalisation of their situation.

The skid row 'alcoholic' who is glamorising his way of life is unlikely to want to change despite what he may say to the contrary. If you are working with him, it is important that you should not back him up in his view by agreeing with his glamorous descriptions of life on skid row. It is just a way in which he can find some self respect and a feeling of direction. However, when it comes to working with a person like this, you will need a considerable amount of tact if you try to suggest a change in his way of life. Without tact, there is a risk that you will be rejected or that you will take away his carefully constructed self respect.

- ## Appearance

Appearance can be deceptive and someone who is sleeping rough or 'skippering' may well make great efforts to keep himself neat and tidy. The way a person looks after himself often says a lot about the way he feels about himself. It is a way in which he can show the world what he is. A 'letting go' or cultivation of a shabby appearance might indicate depression, or that he wants to be identifed as someone who would normally look like this. However, an unkempt, shabby appearance is most often the result of his way of life. What else can be expected when he cannot replace clothes, he is exposed to smutty open fires and he sleeps rough in a 'derrie' (derelict building)?

Where do homeless 'alcoholics' come from?

- **Background to skid row**
  The popular idea that vagrant 'alcoholics' are either romantic, tramp-like figures or ex-professionals down on their luck is rather far from the truth. About 90% of them are semi-skilled or unskilled workers, they are mostly male and used to travelling for work. They are vulnerable to poverty and homelessness to such an extent that they find themselves in an unenviable position. It is often alcohol abuse combined with lack of work or money, or mental illness that finally brings them to a position where they adopt the attitudes and way of life associated with skid row.

  The large number of Scotsmen and Irishmen among skid row drinkers points to a particular problem. Attitudes to alcohol in Scotland and Ireland are often at two extremes: you either drink and drink heavily or you are abstinent. There seems to be little encouragement for anyone who wants to drink moderately, particularly among the lower social classes. This fact is reflected by their very high alcoholism rates.

- **Occupation**
  Links between occupation and alcoholism are well known and high risk occupations are discussed in Chapter 4 of this book. One of those high risk occupations most well represented on skid row is the construction/building industry which is particularly favoured by Scotsmen and Irishmen coming to England in search of work. Workers in this industry rarely have the chance to settle because they often have to be on the move looking for work.

  Another major industry well represented on skid row is catering. Once again, it is an industry which has a high rate of alcoholism. The availability of alcohol can either contribute to someone beginning to abuse alcohol or provide a source of supply for someone with a well-established drink problem. Other common occupational backgrounds for members of skid row are the armed services and seasonal agriculture.

- **Crisis for the 'alcoholic'**

  It is easy to imagine how someone who is dependent on alcohol and regularly drinks large quantities will react when he suddenly finds himself out of work either because of economic recession or because he has become unemployable. He has a heavy drink habit to support and may well decide to give alcohol priority over everything else.

- **Rootlessness**

  The need for mobility in some high risk occupations leaves people with few local roots and few supportive networks such as families and friends who are willing to tide them over difficult periods. When a man arrives in a strange town he will often seek the ready companionship of a pub and he may well have to use a particular public house as a point of contact for new work. He would have little to draw him away from the pub and there are few other places where he might want to spend any money he may earn.

Joining skid row

A lot depends on how aware the 'alcoholic' is of skid row as an alternative way of life. Anyone facing the consequences of worsening alcoholism inevitably goes through a period of examining all the options which are open to him before he eventually decides to adopt a particular way of life. It is either at a time of temporary difficulty or when he arrives penniless in a strange town that an 'alcoholic' will often first discover skid row. The contact is often made at a Salvation Army hostel or a cheap lodging house.

Once the alcoholic sees skid row as an alternative way of life, he may wander in and out of it during future times of difficulty. Eventually, he either decides to leave it or begins to join it for periods which become imperceptibly longer as 'alcoholic' or economic (or both) difficulties increase. Figure 12 shows what can be, for some 'alcoholics', the decline to skid row. Their quality of life gradually deteriorates and they move to cheaper accommodation and generally 'make do' at a lower level. However, they hold on at all times to what they see as an essential base line of survival. At this stage they will have avoided the crises of homelessness and they are not aware of any alternative, and so they will often make considerable efforts (and usually with success) to maintain themselves at this minimum level which does not involve actual homelessness.

Later, through whatever circumstances, they are forced into homelessness. A whole new world suddenly opens up to them and they realise that they have passed through a barrier into an alternative way of life. Although they may well pass back to having their own accommodation in the future, they will now be aware that the alternative of 'homelessness' does not seem so terrible and they will know that an alternative actually exists.

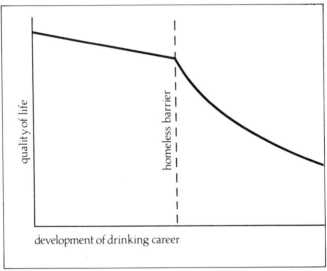

Figure 12: The homeless barrier

An unskilled worker who moves around to find work is more vulnerable and further down the economic scale than someone with local roots or a higher social class. It follows that he is more likely to be exposed to the skid row alternative.

In any event, once somebody has entered the world of skid row, he begins to soak up the atmosphere and skid row will be starting to teach him new attitudes, rules of behaviour and skills for survival. Entry into skid row is a critical point in an 'alcoholic's' career. Not only does he become aware of an alternative life style but he is also able to support his habit of heavy drinking by using new 'tricks of the trade'. He will be introduced to the drinking gang which is designed to make sure alcohol is available for a maximum amount of time by sharing both the resources and the skills needed to acquire it.

It goes without saying that no worker wants to allow someone who is at a point of crisis and homeless for the first time to be exposed to the influence of skid row. If there is any chance of offering treatment for problem drinking it should be offered before it is perhaps too late.

Helping the skid row 'alcoholic'

What happens in practice can be very different from what the helper would like to happen. 'Alcoholics' who are being helped at a critical stage in their drinking career do break through the homeless barrier (see Figure 12) and join skid row, despite the worker's best efforts. As a helper, you might also be asked to help someone direct from skid row. How can you help?

- **How does the homeless 'alcoholic' see alcohol?**
  Before you can start to help anybody who abuses alcohol, you need to understand what benefits the 'alcoholic' feels drink gives him. This is as true of the problem drinker with a home, family and a job as it is of the 'alcoholic' who is single, homeless and poor (see page 162).

  Each 'alcoholic' will see a different series of benefits in his drinking and you need to find out what they are. In fact, for the homeless person on skid row, alcohol gives a degree of direction that little else on skid row offers. Talking about alcohol, buying or stealing alcohol, drinking it and then recovering from its effects take up a considerable amount of time and involve the homeless 'alcoholic' in dealing with other people in a way that gives him a sense of satisfaction.

  Drinking alcohol openly in public shows that the 'drinking gang' is significantly different from other drinkers who drink their alcohol less prominently. Skid row 'alcoholics' are very well aware of how their noisy gathering in a public park sets them apart and makes them a target for police and park keepers. It also feeds their attempts to glamorise their way of life with what they see as elements of 'outlaw' status. As they see it, they are the real drinkers, 'real alkies', whose main priority is downing alcohol. They are not like others who either play around with alcohol or are 'knife and fork "alcoholics" '.

Interestingly, different drinking gangs using different alcoholic beverages see each other in somewhat disparaging terms. Just as the person managing to hang on to a room in a rather more respectable lodging house or Salvation Army hostel looks down upon the 'dossers', so the cheap wine drinker in particular looks down upon smaller, more desperate gangs of crude spirit drinkers, who, in their turn, look down on all the rest because nobody else has their dedication.

The short-term physical effects of alcohol fulfil a very real need to blot out the unpleasant surroundings in which the skid row 'alcoholics' live. Alcohol takes away the guilt for the broken families and the destroyed life that lie in their past and it insulates them from the squalor of their present. A few bottles make sleeping in a derelict 'skipper' on a cold winter's night more bearable, if only because they reduce the numb cold. It is because of these appalling conditions in which they exist that the majority of homeless men suffer more from the consequences of their way of life than from those of alcohol abuse. Frostbite, TB and exposure are more common amongst this community than Korsakoff's syndrome (see page 48).

However, problems which have a close link with alcohol dependence are a real risk for homeless drinkers. Many members of skid row will experience withdrawal symptoms (see page 37) when alcohol is not available. Experience shows that they are most likely to look for outside help at one of these low points in their drinking career. If they turn to you for help, you must be sure that you really want to become involved and that you have a colleague who can support you if the need arises.

- **Working for a change**
  The three main stages in working with the homeless problem drinker are to encourage him to:

  Want to change
  Dare to change
  Try to change

  If you feel unable to cope at any stage, you should contact one of the specialist alcohol agencies (see Appendix 1).

Wanting to change

Unless the 'alcoholic' who has come to look for help wants to change his way of life, there is little anyone can do except offer material assistance.

There are various sources of motivation to change and a perceptive helper can often trigger a desire for improvement by drawing attention to what the homeless 'alcoholic' is doing to himself by his drinking and by his way of life. You need to emphasise the effect that all this is having on him and to point out repeatedly that it is all related to his present predicament.

It must be assumed that anyone who wants to change his identity as a homeless 'alcoholic' feels that it is no longer worth keeping that identity. In other words, there needs to be what is called an identity crisis. This is what most often provokes a skid row 'alcoholic' to want to change and it can be caused by anything from a particularly violent drunken incident to a long, cold, frostbitten night in a 'skipper' with bad withdrawal symptoms in the morning. It can also be caused by a whole series of events that leads him to feel that he can no longer carry on as he is. It is vital that you should be able to recognise these crises and that you are in a position to be able to respond positively.

It is possible for you to foster this critical stage by refusing to give money and material help. This means that the skid row 'alcoholic' will probably not be able to carry on drinking without facing the consequences. An approach like this is often controversial but experience has shown that it can be very successful.

The process of getting a homeless drinker to want to change may be a long one but it is important to keep on trying as long as the 'alcoholic' keeps up the contact. Some helpers may see this long, drawn out process as a failure but, in fact, keeping in touch with the problem drinker and being on hand when an identity crisis happens is the only real source of possible success.

Daring to change

The homeless 'alcoholic' may know that he needs to change his behaviour and his pattern of drinking. He may be well aware of what he is doing to himself, either as a result of a long contact with one or more of the 'caring' professions or as a result of his own experience. Daring to attempt a change is, however, a very different matter.

The 'alcoholic's' attempts to stop drinking and to change his way of life will probably have been dogged by frequent failure. He will often doubt that he can ever achieve any positive difference and it is up to you to decide with him what are realistic options, and to encourage him to attempt what is going to be a difficult programme. It is important not to make the options sound too attractive because a false picture may quickly lead to increasingly bitter disappointment and failure.

Trying to change
Trying to change will often be another long, drawn out process with frequent failure, despair and returns to the old way of life. As before, it is important to persevere and not to write the 'alcoholic' off as being a failure.

The offer of continued help should always be conditional upon the skid row 'alcoholic' wanting to change. It should not be a blanket offer of endless assistance which will tempt him to see you as a source of money and other material support. When you discover you are being used like this, the temptation is to feel betrayed and to consider taking away your help. However, you should bear in mind that successful survival on skid row depends on using any resources that are available. It is better to be alert to the possible 'con' and to avoid being used in the first place.

Alcohol and drug abuse

Although not all the members of skid row you may come across necessarily have a drink problem, they are in a minority. The majority of the men and women who are on skid row do abuse alcohol and many also abuse drugs. They will have obtained these drugs from a variety of sources and the drugs will usually be of the type used to reduce anxiety, which also help to alleviate the symptoms of alcohol withdrawal (see page 40). They may be taken for their own effects or to heighten the effects of alcohol. Skid row sees this misuse of drugs as a perfectly legitimate means of achieving these effects. When a homeless 'alcoholic' denies using drugs, he is usually being wary or is horrified that he might be mistaken for a 'junkie'. In fact, it is rare for men and women on skid row to

abuse drugs such as cannabis, LSD and the opiates traditionally associated with drug abuse.

For anyone helping someone who is vulnerable and in need,
often with a drink problem, success may be simply avoiding
exposure to skid row, because once an 'alcoholic' is on skid
row it becomes much more difficult to work with him,
although it may still be possible to offer help successfully.

No change will be possible, however, unless the 'alcoholic'
wants change and is prepared to make efforts to work towards
it. The task of his helper is to encourage him to want that
change, to direct his efforts and to make appropriate resources
available. It is very important that workers should be prepared
to help because it is very difficult for the single homeless to
fight against their deprivation, their alcohol dependence and
the attitude of society all alone.

7 Assessing the problem drinker

Introduction

Actually identifying alcohol abuse as one of the causes of a person's problems is often no more than the first step in a process which will continue over a period of time. The next step is to offer the 'alcoholic' an assessment interview at his home, in your office or elsewhere (it may be formal or informal, a special appointment or a part of a regular meeting) at which he should feel confident enough to be able to talk about his drink problem at some length. For the interviewer, it is an opportunity to begin to assess what kind of intervention or treatment might be most appropriate and effective.

Some members of the helping professions are often wary of dealing with problem drinkers. They seem to feel that no 'alcoholic' will really change his ways and that, in any case, he is probably inadequate and trying to get something for nothing; worse still, he may be abusive or violent. In fact, taking the trouble to interview a problem drinker properly is usually most rewarding. He may once have been a success as a business man or in the entertainment industry. Invariably, he is such a rich source of life experience that you are left fascinated by him at the end of the interview and yet you remain puzzled as to how drink could have had such a devastating effect on his life. When you think in that way, you want to help; and wanting to help is the essence of being able to help.

First impressions

How you conduct your interview will vary depending on whether or not the person you are interviewing admits he has a drink problem. In either case, the problem drinker will often play down his problem and may try to be rejected by you, the very person to whom he has come to for help. On the other hand, drinking exploits may occasionally be exaggerated out of bravado. Whatever happens it is important to remember that, **given the opportunity, problem drinkers are much more honest than is often believed**.

The interview may be a daunting prospect for the 'alcoholic' and it is useful to tell him that you realise it will be difficult for him to talk freely about drinking. It may make things easier if you emphasise that talking about the problem is the way to get help. You will also need to be aware of the setting: an employer sitting in on the interview may be inhibiting. Any assurances you give must be totally honest. It is all too easy to say, 'This interview is strictly confidential', when a moment's thought tells you that it is nothing of the kind.

Problem drinkers are often quite fragile from a psychological point of view but they have usually set up so many defences that it is easy to underestimate how troubled they really are:

'Fools they thought I was alright
They couldn't see that I was dying inside
Fools don't turn on the light
I can't bear to see their faces
When they see me fall to pieces'

Judie Tzuke

Psychological difficulties and defences

Problem drinkers are often socially isolated, they may be depressed and anxious, they usually feel guilty about past events and almost always have a very low opinion of themselves. This poor self image is sometimes compensated for by exaggerated claims. 'I've got a Black Belt in Judo', followed by a list of would-be helpers who have been 'sorted out' because they could not offer an immediate cure, is typical of the claims made.

Common psychological difficulties of problem drinkers

Poor self image
Lack of identity
Anxiety
Depression
Guilt
Social isolation
(*see Chapters 2 and 3*)

Drinking reverses all of these psychological states; it relieves depression, takes away feelings of guilt and boosts confidence. But there is a rebound effect when drinking stops. The unpleasant psychological effects become all the more intense and lead to continued drinking. However, there is no evidence to suggest that problem drinkers necessarily have any psychological troubles before they start heavy drinking.

In order to keep up their drinking and so relieve their unhappy state of mind, 'alcoholics' will use a number of psychological defences.

- ### Rejection
Problem drinkers may want to be rejected by the helper or to find reasons why they should reject the helper so that they have ample justification to leave the interview and to carry on drinking. The defences used in rejection fall into several categories:

'You're no good, you don't know anything'
At the assessment interview, 'alcoholics' will often test out their would-be helper. Experience has shown that, for example, skid row drinkers will respect you more if you know something about their life style, such as the places where they drink and the language they use (see Chapter 6). It also helps with any drinker if you can talk about the physical effects of alcohol such as withdrawal symptoms and the particular effects it has on health. You also need to phrase your questions in the right way. For example, if you ask, 'What time do you have your first drink of the day?' and get the reply, 'Lunch time', it is worth going on to ask 'Don't you ever have a drink before you get up?'. This may not only yield helpful information, it also shows you know what 'alcoholics' are about.

The point is that if you really do not know what you are doing, then the person you are interviewing is well justified in going elsewhere. If, on the other hand, you are familiar with the subject and the person still leaves saying, 'You're no good', then his need to carry on drinking is probably too great for him to be able to accept any treatment you may recommend anyway.

'You're no good, you're as bad as me'
It is as well to be prepared with an answer in case you are asked, 'Do you drink?'. An honest reply is probably the best.

Even so, the person being interviewed will often try to compare the would-be helper's drinking habits with his own and reach the rather dubious conclusion that there is really very little difference between the two and so, by implication, the helper is no good.

'You're no good, you can't cure me'
Unfortunately, this is often a self-fulfilling prophecy. In many cases, the 'alcoholic' will have already seen a number of people who will have tried, unsuccessfully, to help. It is a defence mechanism which reflects feelings of despair. It may be difficult for the helper not to share the despair. However, it is often a time to be positive and perhaps give direct advice.

- ### Denial and rationalisation
  Denial and rationalisation are different from outright lying because they occur at a subconscious level; the 'alcoholic' really believes what he is telling you. This is sometimes hard to swallow but it is easier if you remember that the problem drinker has probably been telling little lies for years and that he has gradually come to believe more and more of what he has said. Considering the troubles that tend to accumulate in the 'alcoholic's' life, it is hardly surprising that there are attempts to play down the part played by alcohol. As things get worse, alcohol increasingly becomes the only way out.
  Denial is the way the 'alcoholic' maintains psychological stability. Without it, his low opinion of himself would be exposed and he would suffer terrible anxiety. As things go from bad to worse then the greater the problems, the greater the denials. Two short examples illustrate this.

Susan
Susan was a radiographer. She was reported to her head of department because she kept dropping x-rays on the floor. Her explanation? 'I must have taken an extra sleeping tablet'. She was in fact drinking from a bottle of vodka in her locker.

Clive
Clive worked in a foundry where all his workmates were heavy drinkers. Drinking had resulted in Clive losing his wife, accumulating debts and suffering with a stomach ulcer. Clive's view on the possibility that his troubles were due to drink: 'Couldn't be – everyone at work drinks more than I do'.

The full assessment interview

Before you begin your assessment interview, it is worth deciding exactly what questions you want to have answered by the end. These should include:

Assessment questions – Checklist

Does this person really have a drink problem? If so –

Is he mildly, moderately or markedly dependent on alcohol?

What is his level of consumption?

What harm has he done to himself?

What makes him carry on drinking?

What intervention, if any, is appropriate?

It may not be possible to answer all these questions after one interview, particularly if it has not been possible to see a friend or relative to confirm the 'alcoholic's' story. The need to see a friend or relative cannot be overemphasised.

- ### Personal details
  You can glean quite a lot from the information you will probably have on record before seeing the problem drinker. It is known that some groups of people drink more than others.

Personal details Checklist

Age	Most heavy drinkers are between about 25 and 45. They are often likely to develop a serious problem which needs treatment in their late twenties.
Sex	Men are still more likely to be heavy drinkers than women, although there is increasing evidence that more women are beginning to have drinking problems.

Religion	Catholics are often heavy drinkers whereas Muslims and Jews are not.
Marital status	Problem drinkers are more likely to be divorced or separated.
Occupation	Some occupations such as brewing and allied trades, catering, journalism and medicine are associated with problem drinking (see Chapter 4).
Geographic origin	Certain areas of a country have heavy drinking cultures, particularly those where raw materials such as steel and coal are produced.

Using these criteria, it would be no surprise if a 35-year-old, divorced, Irish landlord presented with a drink problem. It would be puzzling if a 22-year-old married Jewish woman who works as a clerk had a drink problem. Looking at this kind of information gives quite a good impression of what sort of case you are dealing with.

- **Present situation**
  A problem drinker can become involved with many different helping agencies. He also seems to have an unusual capacity to throw any referral system into chaos and so it is crucial to be clear exactly what his present circumstances are. If any question seems inappropriate, you should go on to the next one.

Present situation Checklist

Where is the person living? Having nowhere to live may be the problem.

Is the address given correct? Problem drinkers change address frequently.

Is there a telephone number? This may be useful for follow up.

Who referred the person? Be sure you know why you have been asked to see him.

Why does the person think he is seeing you? Often it is because of an accumulation of problems related to drinking and not necessarily the drinking itself.

Is anyone else involved in the case? Social workers or health workers may be involved with the drinker's family. A GP or a psychiatrist may also be involved.

What friends does the person have? No friends or social support may be the problem.

Is the person working? Lack of money, or boredom may be the problem.

Is the person taking any medication? This indicates a contact with medical services. The type of medication may suggest what was thought to be the problem.

- **History and background**
  Having clearly established what the present situation is, it is time to move on to the person's history and background.

History and background Checklist

Social history	*Drinking history*
Family history	Early drinking
Education	Problem drinking
Work record	Drink pattern
Relationships	Withdrawal symptoms
Crime	Good effects
Previous illnesses	Bad effects
Personality	Previous interventions

Social history
Family history: From the family history, it will be helpful to know what the drinking habits and attitudes of the person's

parents were: did they fit in with their social status? If parents were opposed to drinking on moral grounds then remember that drinking can have a symbolic value, especially for young adults, as a way of 'getting at' parents.

Other questions which should be asked are whether the family was a close one, whether aggression was a feature of family life and whether the person was ever living with relatives or in an institution. Psychoanalysts believe that rejection by the family in early childhood can make someone psychologically vulnerable.

If there are any brothers or sisters, do they drink heavily? Is the person you are interviewing the odd one out of the family? If there is a history of psychiatric problems in the family, could this be a reason for the drinking?

Remembering that you are trying to assess what intervention might be made, it is useful to know what contact the person has with his family and whether family members are likely to be supportive, and even involved, in treatment.

Education: The level of the 'alcoholic's' education, including apprenticeships, gives some measure of intelligence. It is then possible to compare expectations for achievement with reality. Important hints at psychological problems that may make the person susceptible to drinking can often be picked up from schooldays. Questions you might consider are whether he had a nickname, whether he rebelled or was a goody goody, and whether he went around with a gang.

Work record: It is useful to make a list of all the jobs the problem drinker has had, together with the dates they were held and the reasons for moving on. An 'alcoholic's' work record often starts off well with promotion to better jobs every year or so, but then, possibly because of increased earnings and more stress at work, drinking starts to interfere. Drinking problems will invariably lead to frequent changes of job and to increasing periods of unemployment.

Always check carefully for any time which may have been spent in high risk occupations (see Chapter 4). If it proves impossible to get many specific answers, even people who have had the most chaotic work record can often be persuaded to remember which job they spent the longest time in and how much time they have spent out of work in the past year.

Relationships: This part of the history tells you something about a person's stability and something about his present state. If he is currently living with someone, then this relationship will be the focus of attention. What is the nature of the relationship? How long have they lived together? Have there been periods of separation? Are there any problems? Is the sexual relationship satisfactory? Are there any children from this or a previous relationship?

Whether or not there is a current relationship you should enquire about previous marriages, the length of previous relationships and the reasons why they broke up. For more information on the importance of the family, see Chapter 3.

Crime: A tactful question such as, 'Have you ever been in trouble?' can introduce this subject. If the answer is, 'Yes', then a list of offences and dates usually makes it clear what kind of person you are dealing with (see Chapter 5).

Previous illness: Again, a tactful question such as, 'Have you ever had any trouble with your nerves?' can indicate psychological problems and lead into asking about physical illness. Both psychiatric and medical problems, especially pain, may trigger or sustain heavy drinking (see Chapter 2).

Personality: It is impossible to make a simple assessment of anyone's personality. However, because the type of treatment to be offered can depend so much upon personality, it is important to try. The following headings may be useful:

- What is the person like in social situations?

- Can he handle one-to-one relationships?

- How does he react to pressure?

- What are his moods like?

- Does he have any particular interest or hobbies?

As an example of why it is so important to try to assess personality, if someone always became aggressive when something he said was challenged, it would probably be best not to recommend any intervention which involved groups.

This general social history will provide background information that will not only be useful when considering what intervention might work but will also give hints, if not strong indications, of what the drinking is all about:

• Is heavy drinking all the person has ever known? If this seems to be the case, it may be difficult to get across that drinking can be harmful.

• Does he have psychological problems that are eased by drinking? If this seems to be the case, then it is probably best to seek specialised help.

• Is the problem drinker someone who was previously well adjusted? If this is the case, it may be possible to identify what has caused the problem and at least to partially reverse it and deal with it.

Drinking history
It is best to deal with the general social history before moving on to deal specifically with drinking. This is because the general social history will often indicate some harm done by drinking and some of the possible causes of continued drinking.

Early drinking: When asked when they started drinking, many problem drinkers will say that it was when they were 16, in a pub. If someone starts drinking at an unusually young or old age, it is worth finding out why. The next question to ask in the interview is about the effect alcohol had on them when they first started drinking. Some people will say they did not like it, others that it made them feel ill or sick but some will have been quickly aware of the drug effect of alcohol. They will have enjoyed getting drunk or drinking made them feel more at ease. These are the people who are perhaps most likely to have developed an early drinking problem.

Problem drinking: It will probably be clear by this time whether or not the person you are interviewing recognises that he has a drink problem. If he does, for how long has he recognised the problem, and why does he believe he has the problem? It is best at this stage just to accept the person's own view of his drinking.

Drinking pattern: There have been many attempts to categorise drinking patterns and to describe them in a few words but none has been really successful. What you need to find out is how much has been drunk and how often it has been drunk. There are so many influences on drinking patterns and it can be so difficult to remember how much was drunk weeks or months ago that the only really worthwhile way of getting information is to start by asking about periods of non-problem drinking:

'Since drinking has been a problem for you, have there been any periods of, say, six months or more when you were drinking a lot less or not at all?' If so, what was the reason?

'In the last year have there been any periods of a week or more when you were drinking moderately or not at all?' If so, what was the reason?

Questions along these lines will not only give a fairly good idea of the pattern of drinking, but might also show what influences help the person to drink less. Some common favourable influences are work, children, wife/husband, girl-friend/boyfriend, lack of money, poor health, a period in hospital or prison, and attending AA or other treatment.

By this stage of the interview, some of the causes and effects of drinking should be clear, but you will still need to find out about 'the last drinking week'. This can usually be remembered in detail and the points to listen out for are the day-to-day variation in drinking, the amount which is drunk and the 'cues' for continued drinking. A useful exercise is to pick a fairly typical day and work through what happens:

Drinking pattern – Checklist

What time do you wake up?

How do you feel in the morning? (Depressed, anxious, irritable?)

Any shakes or sweats?

What time do you have the first drink?

Never a drink before getting up?

How quickly does the first drink go down?

Do you feel better afterwards?

Is drinking fairly steady for rest of the day or in 'top up' sessions?

How much is drunk altogether?

The answers to these questions tell you about the total amount a person drinks in a day and about the withdrawal symptoms he experiences (see Chapter 2). Drinking to get rid of withdrawal symptoms is called 'relief drinking' and it means that having taken a drink to get rid of withdrawal symptoms, these withdrawal symptoms will inevitably return as the blood alcohol level falls. The kind of things people say when they relief drink are:

I need one in the morning to get me going
I pour a drink out at night ready for next morning
The first drink of the day puts me right

The first drink will often be gulped down and relief comes in 15–20 minutes; the actual amount varies but it will probably be a pint of beer or its equivalent.

Once relief drinking is established, there is a vicious circle. Nothing removes the sometimes very unpleasant experience of withdrawal better than alcohol and so drinking has to continue throughout the day to keep up the blood alcohol levels which have become 'normal' for the problem drinker. In other words, he is addicted to alcohol, which means that normal physiological and psychological functions only happen in the presence of a drug, in this case, alcohol.

Withdrawal symptoms: If the problem drinker does not mention withdrawal symptoms such as the shakes, sweats, retching, anxiety, depression or irritability when he talks about his typical day, you should make a point of asking about them at this stage. Always ask about a history of fits or delirium tremens as these indicate that the person will have to be admitted to hospital if he is to be 'dried out' (see Chapter 2).

Good effects of drinking: At some time in the past, if not at present, most problem drinkers felt that alcohol was of some benefit to them. The reasons for this will probably have become apparent by this stage of the interview. It is worth checking that all the reasons have been mentioned and it might be useful to use a few prompts. Was drinking a pleasant social habit? Did it relieve anxiety or depression? Was it a way of escape? Did the drinker enjoy being intoxicated? If someone mentions that one benefit of drinking was that it changed his mood, that might indicate that it will be difficult to find a successful treatment because drinking to change mood is often associated with poor results. It is also worth pointing out that many problem drinkers no longer like the taste of alcohol, they just 'need' it.

Bad effects of drinking: The bad effects of alcohol for the problem drinker are probably also apparent by this time. Again, it is worth checking: are the bad effects of alcohol connected with money, relationships, work, accidents, family, health?

Previous interventions: It is useful to know what help someone has had in the past and you could ask:

- What treatment has and has not been effective before?
- Is there some helper the person you are interviewing relates particularly well?
- Have there been problems during treatment in the past?

The 'alcoholic's' view of previous treatment may be very different to that of whoever was trying to help him. A quick telephone call is often worthwhile. Even if there has been no mention of previous treatment, it is often useful to ring around other helping agencies in the area in order to check.

Assessment supplements

Depending on where the interview takes place and what staff are available, it may be possible to supplement the assessment interview.

- **Questionnaires**
  People vary in their enthusiasm for using questionnaires. There probably is a place for one or two well chosen questionnaires and ones that help evaluate psychological states

137

may be particularly useful for anyone who does not have a background in psychology or psychiatry. Another advantage of using questionnaires is that someone's scores can be compared with future repeats of the questionnaires with the same person in order to assess progress. There is also some evidence that 'alcoholics' are more honest in their response to questionnaires than to an interviewer.

There are very many questionnaires available that may be relevant to assessing problem drinkers, though all of them have their limitations and any would-be user of a questionnaire should be very sure what it is designed to do. The kinds of things that can be measured by questionnaires are dependence on alcohol, anxiety, depression, personality, marital problems and alcohol related problems. The questionnaire included in this section can be used to measure alcohol related problems. It is a questionnaire designed to measure change in someone's way of life over the past year. It is not what is called a screening questionnaire to be filled in by a fairly undefined set of people but it is designed specifically for people who are seeking help with their drinking. It is obvious what the questions are getting at (this is called 'high face validity') and so it would be easy for someone to give untruthful answers if they wanted to, which is what might happen if it was used as a screening questionnaire.

Problems questionnaire

The next few items are to do with problems people commonly experience as a result of drinking. We would like you to circle YES or NO as to whether or not you have experienced the problem in the last year:

1 In the last year have you had any health problems because of drinking? YES   NO

2 In the last year have you gone to anyone for help with your drinking? YES   NO

3 In the last year have you been in hospital because of your drinking? YES   NO

4 In the last year have you moved your job or your home to get away from your drinking problems? YES   NO

5   In the last year have you borrowed money to buy drink?   YES   NO

6   In the last year have you had financial problems because of drink?   YES   NO

7   In the last year have you had trouble or quarrels with your family because of your drinking?   YES   NO

8   In the last year has your wife/husband complained you neglect the family because of your drinking?   YES   NO

9   In the last year have you lost friends or girl/boyfriends because of your drinking?   YES   NO

10   In the last year have you had fights with friends when drinking?   YES   NO

11   In the last year have you lost a job because of your drinking?   YES   NO

12   In the last year have you missed a day's work because of a hangover?   YES   NO

13   In the last year have you been in trouble with the police for a drunkenness offence (other than drinking and driving)?   YES   NO

14   In the last year have you been in trouble with the police for drinking and driving?   YES   NO

15   In the last year have you been in a road accident (as a driver or pedestrian) because of drinking?   YES   NO

16   In the last year have you had an accident at home or work because of drinking?   YES   NO

17   In the last year have you been evicted from a house because you were behind with rent/mortgage?   YES   NO

18	In the last year have any children of yours had problems at school?	YES	NO
19	In the last year have any children of yours seen a psychiatrist, psychologist or social worker?	YES	NO
20	In the last year have you stayed in bed all day because of drinking?	YES	NO
21	In the last year have you neglected your personal appearance because of drinking?	YES	NO
22	In the last year have you been violent to your wife or children when drunk?	YES	NO
23	In the last year have you seriously thought of, or attempted, suicide because of problems caused by drinking?	YES	NO
24	In the last year have you seen a psychiatrist, social worker, clergyman or other person because of an emotional problem in which drinking played a part?	YES	NO
25	In the last year have you been told your memory is damaged because of drinking?	YES	NO
26	In the last year have you had fits of jealousy about a loved one when drinking?	YES	NO
27	In the last year have you had any lasting sexual problems because of drinking?	YES	NO

- **Blood tests**

In a *medical setting* it will be possible to include blood tests in the assessment. The most useful are:

MCV (mean corpuscular volume) – may be raised – reflects drinking over last two to three weeks – result of toxic effect of alcohol on bone marrow.

SGOT (serum glutamic oxalo-acetic transaminase) – may be raised – reflects drinking over last two to three weeks – result of liver damage.

GGT (gamma glutamyl transpeptidase) – may be raised – reflects drinking in last few days – result of liver damage.

Blood alcohol – if the test for blood alcohol is positive it provides a cross check with the patient's history – if the blood alcohol level is very high and the patient does not appear to be intoxicated, it is an indication of tolerance to alcohol.

There are reasons for abnormal blood tests other than drinking and it may be necessary to check these out.

- **Physical examination**
  If a doctor is available then it is possible to include a physical examination in the assessment. The search will usually be for abnormalities in the cardiovascular system (heart and circulation), the liver and for a peripheral neuropathy (damage to the nerves supplying the arms and legs).

The rapid assessment

There are no short cuts to a proper assessment but, for many helpers, a decision may have to be made on the basis of a five or ten minute interview. The objective of rapid assessment is to decide whether a problem drinker needs to be referred to another agency and, if so, which (see Chapter 8).

Checklist

Might alcohol be involved here?

What is the present situation?

Is the person himself or is a friend or relative worried about his drinking?

Is the average daily consumption more than 5 pints of beer or their equivalent (see page 33)?

Is every day a drinking day?

Having taken the first drink or two, is it difficult to stop?

Has the person experienced withdrawal symptoms?

Has there been any previous treatment (including attendance at groups such as Alcoholics Anonymous)?

Just when to raise suspicions about alcohol will be dictated by circumstances. Finding out about the 'present situation' should make it clear why someone is being seen at that particular time. There may be a crisis that needs to be settled before going on or it may be that a crisis means immediate action must be taken. Positive answers to any of the remaining questions on the checklist confirm that drinking may well be a serious problem which needs to be looked at in greater depth.

There are a number of aspects to assessment. It is a time when someone is encouraged to talk about himself, perhaps for the first time. This alone can often be an effective way of getting someone to change his drinking habits and his way of life. It probably helps if you reinforce the assessment with educational handouts.

If a full assessment is made right at the beginning, there is the best chance of making the right decision about what to do. Whatever treatment or intervention is chosen can be put into action as soon as possible. It is not easy to make an assessment and the skills of interviewing can only be learned effectively with practice. So much in assessment is based on the intuitive feelings of the helper and on his knowledge of what resources are available locally that there is no substitute for experience.

If there is ever any doubt as to what intervention to recommend to a problem drinker, and there are no colleagues to turn to for advice, it is always a good idea to contact the local Alcohol Advice Centre (see Appendix 1) which is there to offer specialised help.

8 *Options for treatment*

Introduction

Any drinking problem needs to be dealt with in three stages and two of the three have already been discussed. The first is *detection* (Chapters 2–6) when drinking is identified as one of the causes of a person's problems. The second is *assessment* (Chapter 7), when a problem drinker is interviewed and given the chance to talk about himself and his drinking. The aim of assessment is to try to decide, often in consultation with the 'alcoholic' himself, what might be the most appropriate and effective treatment to offer him at the third stage, *intervention*, which is the subject of this chapter and chapters 9 and 10.

It is worth stressing here that if anyone who detects a problem drinker does not feel able to make an assessment (and it is something which requires skill and sensitivity), it is possible to refer him directly to the local Alcohol Advice Centre. The staff there will be able to assess the problem and recommend an appropriate intervention. On the other hand, if you do decide to make your own assessment, there is a wide range of services available to 'alcoholics' which you will need to know about if the intervention you recommend is to be the most effective one.

Who helps the problem drinker?

Services for problem drinkers Checklist

Alcohol Advice Centres (local or regional Councils on Alcoholism)

National Health Service Alcohol Treatment Units and Addiction Units

NHS Outpatient Clinics

NHS Medical wards and General psychiatric hospitals

Alcoholics Anonymous, Al-Anon and Alateen

- ### *Alcohol Advice Centres*
  There is a network of Alcohol Advice Centres throughout the country and most of them are administered by the local or regional Council on Alcoholism. There is also a wide range of agencies, such as ACCEPT and the Alcohol Counselling Service, based in London.

  Alcohol Advice Centres will always be glad to offer help and advice and to put you in touch with services which are available in your local area. As a general guide, Alcohol Advice Centres can usually provide:

  General advice on alcohol problems

  Assessment and interview facilities

  Individual, marriage and family counselling (Sometimes one counselling session can be all that is needed.)

  Educational groups which discuss a wide range of relevant topics (see Chapter 10)

  Therapeutic groups, in which problem drinkers are encouraged to talk about their feelings and about their reactions to one another and to treatment

  Referral for treatment to other services

  Aftercare support, which is provided when initial treatment has been given by some other service

  An Alcohol Advice Centre will also know about all the other facilities for 'alcoholics' which are available in the area. In addition, some of the centres provide a 'casework consultancy' service. This means that the Alcohol Advice Centre provides support and advice to other workers such as probation officers, clergymen, welfare officers and social workers who are attempting to help someone with a drink problem.

  Another function of the Alcohol Advice Centres is to try to prevent problem drinking by making the people who live in their areas more aware of the effects that alcohol can have and of topics such as drinking and driving, heavy drinking and underage drinking. Staff are often pleased to be invited to talk at schools, clubs and anywhere people meet.

145

- **National Health Service Alcohol Treatment Units and Addiction Units**
The first regional Alcohol Treatment Unit (ATU) was established in the early fifties at Warlingham Park in Surrey and the number of units grew steadily until the early seventies. Obviously, ATUs differ in their approaches to treatment but the basic objective, which is to provide specialist inpatient treatment for drinking problems, remains the same. The approach at Scalebor Park is fairly typical of ATUs.

Scalebor Park ATU
People who end up in Alcohol Treatment Units are not unselected. The patient has to select himself by agreeing to consider total abstinence from alcohol as an aim of his treatment. There is also the selection which happens in the outpatients' department, where the therapists detect a drink problem and the patient appears to accept the proposed treatment in hospital. Finally, after a patient is admitted to hospital, there is a period of two weeks during which the staff assess how well he responds to educational counselling and how well he complies with hospital rules.

Hospital rules

No drinking or taking unprescribed drugs
Frankness in discussing personal problems
Mutual trust and confidentiality between members of the group
Remaining within hospital grounds for seven days
Following the timetable of hospital activities such as group sessions, meals, bedtimes, etc

---

All patients are given an information sheet describing the treatment programme as soon as they are admitted to hospital and are also given a thorough physical examination including a chest x-ray, a full blood count and liver function tests as well as intelligence tests.

During these two weeks which follow admission, each person is assessed in terms of his personality, and of how he gets along with other members of the group, with staff and with his family. By means of this initial assessment, it is possible to avoid the pointless treatment of patients who are unwilling to consider changing both their drinking habits and part or all of their way of life. People with certain personality disorders of any severity are also considered unsuitable for this type of treatment because they are seldom able to cope with the frank exchanges which happen in group therapy sessions (see Chapter 10).

One of the virtues of an initial two weeks' assessment is that the bad impressions created by someone when he is drunk may entirely disappear once he is sober. This means that therapy can be offered with more confidence.

If further treatment is offered, it consists of six weeks of group therapy and individual counselling. Other treatment, such as anxiety management and behavioural psychotherapy may also be provided by the clinical psychologist. Of the smaller number of patients refused admission, some may make an effort to stop drinking by going along to meetings of Alcoholic Anonymous where they receive long-term support from a 'recovering alcoholic'. Others continue to destroy themselves either by the physical complications of continued drinking or by successful attempts at suicide.

During treatment, patients are encouraged to have visitors such as close friends and relatives, who can also be seen by the staff if necessary. After the first two weeks, weekends at home are encouraged to test how motivated the patient is to stay sober and to assess any change in his relationships with his family or friends.

The atmosphere in the hospital ward is friendly, relaxed and informal, and a variety of facilities is available to keep the patients' minds occupied. 'Alcoholics' who have stopped drinking recently are often thirsty, so there is always an ample supply of tea and coffee available. Patients can also cook snacks in the ward kitchen. In fact, cooking is an important skill that often needs to be relearned if a patient is going to survive on discharge.

For all patients, whether the results of their treatment are successful or not, Scalebor Park offers organised weekly follow up groups. This is done because it was noticed that nearly all patients became very anxious as the last day of their stay in hospital approached. The idea that support would continue to be available often seemed to ease these anxieties. Individual counselling is available at these weekly meetings as well as large, open groups.

Apart from these organised weekly sessions, ex-patients and their relatives are also allowed to contact a member of staff with whom there has been particularly close relationship. The different styles and personalities of the five nurses, two doctors and one social worker allow the patients and ex-patients to select a particular therapist whose services they can call on either regularly or intermittently over a period of months or even years.

If assessment indicates that admission to an Alcohol Treatment Unit would be the best form of intervention, you should make an approach direct to the consultant psychiatrist at the unit. It is only on rare occasions that the units will insist on a referral from a family doctor.

Addiction Units work on a similar basis to the Alcohol Treatment Units but, as the name implies, treatment is also offered for addiction to substances other than alcohol.

- **NHS outpatient clinics**
  Not all 'alcoholics' require admission to hospital. Most hospitals have medical staff with some knowledge of drinking problems. When admission is not necessary, or in areas where ATUs or other specialist facilities are not available, patients will be seen as outpatients by psychiatrists and psychologists who will supervise them as they 'dry out' and begin appropriate treatment.

- **NHS medical wards and general psychiatric hospitals**
  Problem drinkers frequently seek help in a crisis when treatment is needed so urgently that even a rapid assessment is impossible. Patients of this type often need treatment for DTs or a serious physical illness (see Chapter 2) and they may be referred to a medical ward in a general hospital. When someone needs urgent help like this, he should be taken first to the Accident and Emergency Department of the hospital.

  General psychiatric hospitals often admit problem drinkers for a short period of time (one to three weeks) and referrals may be made through the duty psychiatrist. It is helpful if patients can be escorted to the hospital and if the person who refers them can write a short letter which outlines the circumstances of the case. The results of this type of treatment are improved when contact can be maintained with the patient and provision made to support him when he leaves hospital.

  In some medical settings, drugs are used to help a problem drinker remain abstinent. Disulfiram (trade name *Antabuse*) and citrated calcium carbide (trade name *Abstem*) are both drugs which block the normal breakdown of alcohol and cause a build up of a toxic chemical, acetaldehyde, in the blood. This induces violent flushing, racing of the heart, headache and vomiting. The idea is that if a patient takes either of these drugs, he knows that he will feel very ill if he drinks. This form of treatment should always have adequate medical supervision since patients often drink even though they are taking *Antabuse* or *Abstem* and there may be only a slightly unpleasant reaction between alcohol and the drug. On the other hand, the drug-alcohol reaction may be severe and so caution is advised. Anyone who is to take either of the drugs must be physically fit and be careful not to take vinegar or tonics which sometimes react with the drugs in a similar way to drink.

- **Alcoholics Anonymous, Al-Anon and Alateen**
  Alcoholics Anonymous has a large number of groups throughout Great Britain. AA members aim to stop drinking and to remain sober by meeting together with other people who share the same problem. Part of the scheme of AA is to 'help other sufferers' and when AA members have achieved a period of sobriety, they do everything they can to help other 'alcoholics' who turn to AA for help.

  Alcoholics Anonymous has been functioning in the USA (where it was founded) since 1935 and the first group was established in this country in the late forties. It is widely seen as one of the most successful self-help groups and a lot was learned from AA in the early development of clinical treatment for problem drinkers.

  The AA programme is based on 12 steps:
  1 We admitted we were powerless over alcohol – that our lives had become unmanageable.
  2 Came to believe that a power greater than ourselves could restore us to sanity.
  3 Made a decision to turn our will and our lives over to the care of God as we understand Him.
  4 Made a searching and fearless moral inventory of ourselves.
  5 Admitted to God, to ourselves and to another human being the exact nature of our wrongs.
  6 Were entirely ready to have God remove all these defects of character.

7 Humbly asked Him to remove our shortcomings.
8 Made a list of all persons we had harmed, and became willing to make amends to them all.
9 Made direct amends to such people wherever possible, except when to do so would injure them or others.
10 Continued to take a personal inventory, and when we were wrong, promptly admitted it.
11 Sought through the power of prayer and meditation to improve our conscious contact with God as we understand Him praying only for knowledge of His will for us and the power to carry that out.
12 Having had a spiritual awakening as the result of these steps, we tried to carry this message to alcoholics and to practise these principles in all our affairs.

The objectives of AA are embodied in the 12 traditions:
1 Our common welfare should come first; personal recovery depends upon AA unity.
2 For our group purpose there is but one ultimate authority – a loving God as He may express Himself in our group conscience. Our leaders are but trusted servants; they do not govern.
3 The only requirement for AA membership is a desire to stop drinking.
4 Each group should be autonomous except in matters affecting other groups or AA as a whole.
5 Each group has but one primary purpose – to carry its message to the alcoholic who still suffers.
6 An AA group ought never endorse, finance or lend the AA name to any related facility or outside enterprise, lest problems of money, property and prestige divert us from our primary purpose.
7 Every AA group ought to be fully self-supporting, declining outside contributions.
8 Alcoholics Anonymous should remain forever non-professional, but our service centres may employ special workers.
9 AA as such, ought never be organised; but we may create service boards or committees directly responsible to those they serve.
10 Alcoholics Anonymous has no opinion on outside issues; hence the AA name ought never be drawn into public controversy.

11 Our public relations policy is based on attraction rather than promotion; we need always to maintain personal anonymity at the level of press, radio and films.
12 Anonymity is the spiritual foundation of all our traditions, ever reminding us to place principles before personalities.

One of the advantages of Alcoholics Anonymous is that there are no referral criteria, no appointments needed and no detailed histories taken. It is completely confidential and anonymous and very little is expected of people attending meetings. First names only are used.

The process of recovery, through AA, is based on the principles of:

Sharing
Self evaluation
Admission of defects
Identification
Making reparation
Helping others
Honesty

Newcomers to AA meetings usually have a 'sponsor' who looks after them at their first meeting and acts as a friend and listener when things are going wrong. The sponsor, usually someone who has been dry for some time, will encourage the new member to attend meetings and help him to overcome early anxiety.

One of the disadvantages of AA for some people is its group atmosphere. Some people find it very difficult to cope with this and others find it difficult to cope with the 'spiritual' content. AA groups often hold 'Open Meetings' about once a month which anybody can attend to find out more about how AA works.

The local AA group can usually be contacted by telephone (under Alcoholics Anonymous in the telephone directory) or by getting in touch with your local Citizens' Advice Bureau or the Samaritans.

Al-Anon, now a separate organisation, began as an offshoot group of AA and aims to provide support, by holding meetings for the partners, other family members and friends of problem drinkers. Al-Anon usually meets in the same building as AA and, in some cases, the drinker goes to the AA meeting at the same time as his partner goes to the Al-Anon meeting. It is not necessary to know someone who goes to AA before going to Al-Anon. Many people have derived great support from Al-Anon when they were driven to desperation by their partner's continued drinking. As with AA, complete anonymity is maintained and the principles of *sharing, identification and support* apply in exactly the same way.

Alateen works on similar principles to Al-Anon and provides support for young adults whose parents are problem drinkers. Alateen groups are not as widespread as those of Al-Anon but they are continuing to expand.

- ### Hostel and residential facilities
  There are many organisations throughout the country which provide hostel and residential accommodation for problem drinkers (see Appendix 1). They fall into five main categories:

Dry houses
Halfway houses
Salvation/Church Army hostels
Night shelters
Government resettlement units (Reception centres)

Dry houses
It has been fairly widely accepted that abstinence is what many 'alcoholics' have to aim at and voluntary organisations have set up a number of residential establishments in various parts of the country with this aim in mind. The way in which these 'dry houses' operate varies from area to area but most of them cater for small groups of people. The rules are few and the commitment of the resident is usually to:

- Remain abstinent.

- Attend group meetings to discuss domestic and personal matters.

- Participate in the running of the house.

Many dry houses also encourage residents to look for work after they have had a reasonable period of abstinence.

The degree of staff involvement varies widely. Some 'dry houses' have a worker who lives in whilst others have workers who visit only on specific days. Someone from the Probation Service, such as the homeless offenders' officer, will usually be in touch with the staff of the 'dry houses' in the area.

If a 'dry house' is the intervention chosen after discussion with the problem drinker, the first approach may be made to the local probation office.

Halfway houses
Halfway houses are usually most suitable for people who have been receiving some form of hospital treatment and need a continuation of their treatment back in the community before they set out to live on their own once again. The local Alcohol Advice Centre will provide information on admissions.

Salvation/Church Army hostels
The Salvation Army and the Church Army have many hostels which house a large number of people. They cater for all types of single homeless people and are willing to accept problem drinkers. However, these hostels may sometimes be a point of contact with skid row 'alcoholics' (see Chapter 6).

Night shelters
There are many night shelters, particularly in large cities, which provide warmth, food and basic accommodation. However, since they are often used by homeless problem drinkers, they may once again be a point of contact with skid row.

Government resettlement units
Formerly known as Reception Centres, these units are administered by the Department of Health and Social Security. They are willing to accept homeless problem drinkers and are often in liaison with local treatment facilities. Unfortunately, they may be yet another contact point for skid row 'alcoholics'.

This list of services which are available to problem drinkers is not exhaustive. For example, a number of day centres for problem drinkers has been established and more are planned. The list is intended to give an idea of the facilities which are available nationally.

For a comprehensive list of projects, you should consult the *Directory of Projects* (England and Wales). Details of how to get hold of a copy of the Directory can be found in Appendix 1.

Setting up an Alcohol Advice Centre in your area

If your work involves dealing with problem drinkers at all frequently, you will quickly get to know the facilities which are available to them in your area. Most people seem to find that the local Alcohol Advice Centre (or its equivalent) becomes a regular source of help because, in most cases, it is probably the organisation which is best able to offer a comprehensive range of services. However, if there is no Alcohol Advice Centre in your town or city, establishing one could be a priority and you, whoever you are, could be the driving force behind the whole project. How?

The first question to ask is exactly what sort of a centre you want to provide. One which offers a counselling service would help to deal with a limited number of cases of problem drinking but it would do nothing to prevent those problems happening in the first place. If you want to increase general awareness of alcohol related problems, to improve facilities and to make sure that more people such as doctors, health visitors, school teachers, social workers and clergymen are able to spot a drink problem, any project you think about trying to set up should also include an advice and education service.

Once you have decided that you are prepared to make the effort and the sacrifices you will undoubtedly have to make to set up a new Alcohol Advice Centre, the next step is to arouse the interest of colleagues and friends who might share your enthusiasm. It is often worthwhile trying to find someone who has a lot of spare time such as a recently retired doctor or social worker.

After you have found some support, you will need to visit some neighbouring areas which have already established a service to find out how they went about it. People seem to like talking about how they have set up their facilities and enjoy passing on any information to other people who show an interest. You will also need to do quite a lot of background reading so that you can formulate your ideas and set them down on paper.

It is also useful to try and discover approximately how many people will use the facilities you hope to provide. To give a rough idea, the Office of Population Censuses and Surveys estimated in 1977 that about 1.3% of the adult population had a drink problem. If the population of your area is, for instance, 200,000, then 75% of these people are likely to be adult which is 150,000. If 1.3% of them are problem drinkers, this would give a figure of 1,950. You can also base your estimate of the potential users of your service on local figures for:

Deaths due to cirrhosis
Drunkenness convictions
Drinking and driving convictions
Admissions to hospital for problem drinking

Other agencies in your area which should be able to give you an idea of the numbers of cases of problem drinking they have dealt with are:

Social Services
Probation Service
Samaritans
Marriage Guidance Council
Police
GPs
Health visitors

A useful way to stimulate interest and awareness in the early stages is to organise a training day on alcohol (see Chapter 13). You should invite people whose support you see as crucial to the success of your project and the speakers should be experienced and skilled specialists who can talk interestingly about their work and about the projects (similar to the one you hope to set up) in which they are involved.

If the training day is successful, the next step is to invite all those who attended it to a public meeting to discuss plans for the development of services for the problem drinker. The best people to ask to act as joint chairmen at the meeting are a member of the Health Authority and a member of the Council's Social Services Committee. Other people you should invite, provided they are likely to help you, are:

Regional/local consultant psychiatrist
Clinical psychologist
Assistant chief or senior probation officer
Director of Social Services
Hospital social worker
Community affairs police inspector

Health education officer
Magistrate(s)
Hospital sister or charge nurse
General practitioner
Member of Alcoholics Anonymous
Solicitor
Accountant
Banker
Clergyman

If the public meeting is successful, you should try to ensure that these people take their place on a working party which will examine the possibility of developing a local Council on Alcoholism (Alcohol Advice Centre).

Once it has been agreed to set up a local Council on Alcoholism, you need to find funding for the project. To begin with, you may be able to raise the money through donations from churches, industry, charitable trusts and individuals. Other local organisations will often help with typing, duplicating and mailing. If a decision is made to attempt to open an Alcohol Advice Centre to the public, you can either develop a voluntary counselling, advice and education service or, if sufficient funds are available, it may be possible to recruit a full time worker. Possible sources of funding for a full time worker are:

Local authority
Health authority
Charitable trusts
Fund raising
DHSS via National Council on Alcoholism
Inner city joint funding
Manpower Services Commission Project

Maintaining funding for a Council on Alcoholism is always a constant battle and it is important to have the support of councillors and members of the Health Authority.

The services offered by local Councils on Alcoholism vary widely and they are designed to meet local needs. However, most of them can offer the following services to a greater or lesser degree:

Advice service
Information
Counselling problem drinkers and families

Contact with hospital services
Education
Providing speakers for meetings
Coordination of services for problem drinkers
Aftercare support
Setting up residential facilities
Advice to industry
Research

Voluntary counselling

If you want to organise training for voluntary counsellors, other local Councils on Alcoholism should be able to give you the benefit of their experience. If you would like to train as a voluntary counsellor yourself, your local Council on Alcoholism, if there is one, or the National Council on Alcoholism should be able to advise you of suitable training courses and of organisations which may be able to use your services.

Change is inevitably a gradual process. Ideas about how to treat alcoholism and problem drinking fluctuate and the present trend is towards early identification of the problem and towards providing community-based treatment. A recent government advisory commission recommended that, 'places' should be set up in the community which would be staffed by a mixture of medical, nursing and social work staff as well as voluntary counsellors. These 'places' would act as a focal point for future education, treatment and research.

9 Which route – abstinence or control?

Introduction

One question often asked about the treatment of problem drinkers who do not need to be supervised by a hospital team is, 'Who should do the treatment?' The answer might be, 'Whoever wants to', and so the main purpose of this chapter is to suggest a few ways in which caring professionals like GPs, social workers, health visitors, probation officers and community nurses who come into contact with alcohol problems in their day-to-day work can offer effective treatment.

The chapter should also help anybody who is confronted with the problems of living or working with an 'alcoholic'. All too often wives and husbands, parents and children, workmates and friends feel impotent when someone close to them clearly needs practical help and advice.

Ways of detecting and assessing a drink problem have been dealt with in earlier parts of this book. It is important to remember in every case that alcoholism can be associated with some very disturbing physical and mental conditions. If you ever feel that anything might be seriously wrong, you should contact someone who specialises in dealing with 'alcoholics' immediately (see Appendix 1).

Once you decide to help a problem drinker, one of the first things you will need to do is to agree with him on what is called a treatment goal. For many years, it was thought that an 'alcoholic' could never drink again. Total abstinence was seen as the only possible treatment goal and phrases like 'once an 'alcoholic' always an 'alcoholic',' or, 'one drink, one drunk', came to be treated as facts. It was argued that any 'alcoholic' who was able to drink moderately after treatment was not an 'alcoholic' in the first place.

Despite this argument, experience has shown that some 'alcoholics' do seem to be able to return to moderate social drinking even after long periods of alcohol abuse. Nevertheless, there is no question that for many, probably most, 'alcoholics', total abstinence is the only possible way of tackling the future.

It is likely that some problem drinkers are deterred from seeking help because they feel that a lifetime without drink is impossible in their particular way of life. On the other hand, they may seek help and really want to sort the problem out but, because they want to work towards moderate drinking, they will be rejected by treatment programmes which demand total abstinence. There is no doubt that a controlled drinking goal cannot be embarked upon lightly and many issues need to be considered by both the drinker and the helper. These will be discussed in more detail later. However, it needs to be said at the outset that the most effective way to treat any illness or problem is to fit the treatment to the needs of the client rather than the other way round.

Six steps to harm-free drinking

For many people who have to face a drink problem, harm-free drinking must mean total abstinence and their way of life will need to be modified accordingly. There should be a commitment to remove alcohol from their life completely. For a few, harm-free drinking can be taken to mean moderate controlled drinking. It has been estimated that about 5 pints of beer (or their equivalent) a day can be potentially damaging to health and so controlled drinking would mean drinking less than this.

Whichever of the treatment goals is chosen, there is a number of planned strategies which will help both the problem drinker and the person who is working with him. In the tradition of Alcoholics Anonymous, these strategies can be seen as steps.

Six steps to harm-free drinking Checklist

Step 1 Admitting the problem and making a commitment to change
Step 2 Thinking specifically about the good effects of alcohol
Step 3 Thinking specifically about the bad effects of alcohol
(Step 4 Going back to the community)
Step 5 Maintaining a drinking goal
Step 6 Dealing with slip ups

- *Step 1: Admitting the problem and making a commitment to change*

Some 'alcoholics', no matter how obvious their difficulties, manage to convince themselves that everyone else is being over-sensitive and that there is really no problem at all. They deny or rationalise their drinking behaviour and you can imagine how they will begin their first conversation, 'I drink the same as all my mates', 'I just came because the wife sent me', or, 'The foreman said I would get the sack if I came in drunk again. But I haven't got a drink problem'. Not every problem drinker is like this and some will come straight out and ask for your help. The outlook for these people is very much better. Once someone admits that there is a problem it makes him alert to the reality of the situation.

Making a personal commitment to change his drinking habits is perhaps the most crucial step a problem drinker takes. It not only means that he is willing to accept help but there is also evidence to suggest that once a commitment has been made, he is even more keen for the treatment to succeed.

It can be difficult for some people to make a commitment at first because, even when they want to give up drinking, part of them seems determined to make them carry on drinking. The best way to resolve this indecision or conflict and to encourage problem drinkers to want to stop drinking is to try to get them to agree to a treatment programme, perhaps by using Steps 2 and 3 of this section.

Just how and when someone's mind accepts commitment can be puzzling. Sometimes it can be related to a crisis or to serious physical problems, but it is just as likely to happen out of the blue. This period of commitment can be a time of euphoria, boundless confidence and jubilation because it seems that there is a miracle cure after all. Whoever is involved in helping the problem drinker must be careful to avoid being sucked into this emotional whirlpool and must realise that all that has happened is that a decision has been made to do something about drinking; nothing has actually been done.

- *Step 2: Thinking specifically about the good effects of alcohol*

It is better to write down a list of the good effects of alcohol than just to think about them. This can help to clarify everyone's thoughts because the typical problem drinker has only a vague idea about the effects of his drinking. It may appear counter-productive at first to list the drinking pros, but even the most harmful drinking behaviour continues because it produces short term gains for the drinker. This is called re-inforcement. Grouping the effects under headings such as changes of mood, feelings of escape and social and physical effects may be useful.

- **Step 3: Thinking specifically about the bad effects of alcohol**
  In this case, the headings could include the effects on the drinker's image of himself, on his family life, marriage, work, finance and his physical health. It helps to keep going back to the list from time to time and to keep on adding to it. The next stage is to compare the lists of good effects (pros) and bad effects (cons) and to set them out as a kind of balance sheet (see Figure 13).

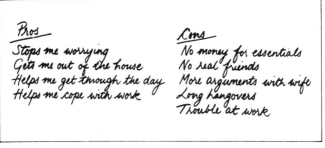

Figure 13: Drinking balance sheet

It is possible to go on to draw up what is called a 'Drinking Decision Matrix' (see opposite page). It is not the actual number of items on each list which decides the balance but the importance attached to each one.

During counselling or other treatment, more effects can be added to the lists and the problem drinker can work out in detail what he has got to gain and lose by changing his drinking habits. At this stage, treatment should be aimed at helping the 'alcoholic' to cope with the effects which not drinking is having on him and to reduce the 'losses'. For example, if one of the good effects of alcohol has been a decrease of tension, then relaxation training could be given to compensate for the tension that will be felt when not drinking. If the 'alcoholic' begins to feel less confident about coping with life, it might be worthwhile discussing and practising various social skills (see page 184). If he has nowhere to go in the evening now he no longer goes to the pub then it might be worth considering alternative activities such as taking up a sport or going to evening classes.

	Stop drinking	Continue drinking
Positive outcomes (good effects)	More respect from others	Remain 'one of the boys'
	Feel better physically	Temporary anxiety relief
	More money	
Negative outcomes (bad effects)	Nowhere to go	Divorce
	Less confidence	Sack
		Liver damage
		Depression

Figure 14: Drinking decision matrix

• **(Step 4: Back to the community)**
Most people find it relatively easy to stop drinking and to remain sober when they are receiving treatment in hospital. If they are going to start drinking heavily again, this is most likely to happen when they return to their family and friends. When no real changes have taken place in the person and in those closest to him, it is more than likely that he will go back to his old drinking habits.

A useful way to get problem drinkers to think about how things will be when they return home is to get them to answer short questions on a number of Checklists.

'Self' Checklist

What kind of person am I?
How would I like to be?

What can I do to change things?
What aspects of my personality and behaviour need changing?

The problem drinker should list specific changes he would like to see in himself and ways in which he thinks he can put them into operation. If he sees himself as an ill, hopeless drunk who has an uncontrollable urge to drink alcohol he will probably end up like that. It is more productive if he begins to see himself as someone who is responsible for his own future and who can actively change his way of life. Experience has shown that if there is a move from external control ('I am ill and I need treatment') to internal control ('I am responsible for my own destiny'), then it is a positive sign of improvement. After completing the 'self' checklist, it is useful for a problem drinker to examine his role as a parent and husband.

'Family' Checklist

How exactly am I seen by my wife/daughter/son?
Why am I seen in this way?
How would I like to be seen?
How can I work towards this?
How do I want the members of my family to change their behaviour towards me?
Will my family change?

At this stage it can be helpful to hold discussions between husband and wife and, sometimes, children. 'Will my family change?' is a question which needs some thought. It does not follow that a family will change its behaviour when the 'alcoholic' cuts down or stops his drinking. An example may explain this more clearly.

Brian
Brian has been a heavy drinker for many years and his situation has gradually become intolerable. He has lost his job and spends most of his time in the house or the pub. Over the years, his wife, who has become the breadwinner, has assumed responsibility for the children and the finances, and organises what social life is left. She has often been on the point of leaving Brian but has returned when

he promised, unsuccessfully, to give up drinking. Brian has eventually come into hospital with severe withdrawal symptoms but, like Aesop's boy who called 'wolf', no-one in his family now believes he will stop drinking. Despite his motivation to stop on this occasion, it is unlikely that Brian's wife will ever trust him with responsibility.

Joint counselling may help them to begin building up trust and being in hospital means that Brian can practise social skills which he has lost over the years such as managing money, job hunting and DIY. Continued counselling may help his wife to give Brian back some of his old responsibilities which she has begun to enjoy. In this way Brian will begin to see himself in a favourable light.

As the drinker changes his general behaviour, other members of the family also need to change. If an 'alcoholic' has to go into hospital a helper can work with the family and also offer follow-up support. In cases where hospital treatment is not needed it is equally important for whoever is helping the problem drinker to keep in touch with his family and friends. Re-adjusting to life with someone who was a problem drinker can be difficult.

Similar checklists to those on 'Self' and 'Family' can be devised to discover how the 'alcoholic' sees himself (and how he feels he is seen by others) in his social life and at work.

● ***Step 5: Maintaining a drinking goal***
If a problem drinker is to maintain his drinking goal over any length of time, he will need to be aware of the signals and situations which make him want to drink or to drink too much. All of us who enjoy a drink, whether problem drinkers or not, experience these signals and situations which make us want to have a drink. The club after a football or rugby match is a good example of a situation for drinking and there are a considerable number of signals which make us want a drink. It is early evening and we are thirsty, there is the smell of the pub or club, there are the intense discussions about why the match was won or lost and, as it is just after payday, there is no shortage of money. After a few pints of beer there is that pleasant feeling of slight intoxication which is a powerful signal to carry on drinking. The surroundings are comfortable and some people have bought in rounds and so we feel that we must buy them drinks in return. Some of the signals which make us want to drink at the football or rugby club are common to many other drinking situations.

Biological state	hunger, thirst, initial effect of alcohol
Emotional state	elation, tension, depression
The time of day	lunch time, evening
The place	smell, sounds, dimmed lighting, comfort
Availability of money and drink	payday, off-licences, supermarket, pub, club
The people you are with	buying rounds, they are critical if you do not drink, good conversation

Different signals are more powerful for different people. The 'alcoholic' however, is influenced not only by all of these signals but also by some additional ones. For example, some 'alcoholics' can wake up in the morning suffering from withdrawal symptoms such as sweats, the shakes and perhaps a feeling of sickness. This is an unpleasant state but the problem drinker has learned from past experience that a drink can relieve these symptoms in about 15 to 20 minutes. It has also been shown that as the 'alcoholic' becomes more dependent on alcohol, signals associated with withdrawal symptoms become increasingly strong.

Using the headings from the 'Signals to drink Checklist' the problem drinker should write down the cues which tempt him to drink too much. The list should be specific rather than vague. For example, under the heading, 'The place', it is better to write 'The Rose and Crown, because it is comfortable, local and yet private', rather than just 'Pub'. Under 'Emotional state', rather than writing 'Tension', it may be useful to write down some of the things which cause the tension, such as 'After yet another row with wife/husband', 'After criticism at work', or 'Being with a particular group of people'. The more specific the signals, the easier it is to discuss practical ways of reducing their influence.

The next stage is for the problem drinker and the person who is working with him to list other things he can do when he feels that he needs a drink. Using the headings from the Checklist, some suggestions might be those given below.

Biological state
Thirst: Drink a lot of water or milk which are better thirst quenchers than alcohol.
Hunger: Begin to have a regular meal routine.

Emotional state
Tension: Be more assertive at work, settle arguments with partner.
Social frustration: Concentrate on re-learning social skills, such as saying 'no', using the correct tone of voice and telling jokes.

Time of day
Lunch time drinking: Arrange to go home at lunch time or to mix with colleagues who go to the canteen rather than to the pub. Avoid the pub on weekdays or paydays.

The place
Pub: Enrol at evening classes, take up squash, go out with wife or husband to the cinema once a week, begin following serials on TV.

Availability of money/drink
Money: Avoid carrying cash or let wife/husband control spending money. Get your wage paid directly into bank account

People you are with
Drinking friends: Spend more time with the people you have told about the problem and who do not pressure you to drink

This is by no means an exhaustive list and it will be different for everyone. In order to reduce the problem drinker's chances of returning to heavy drinking, it is clear that a great deal of work needs to be done to alter his day to day routine and his whole way of life. The ultimate aim is to produce permanent changes which will reduce the risk of drinking (or renewed heavy drinking if the treatment goal is controlled drinking).

- **Step 6: Dealing with slip-ups**
  It always seems that some problem drinkers start off with good intentions but that the pressures both within and around them can lead them to take up drinking again. However, it is most important that one slip-up is not regarded either as a failure or as an excuse to give up hope and go back to full

time drinking. A problem drinker needs to be able to admit that he has slipped and to talk about it either with professionals or with his friends or family. It is useful if he has a list of names, addresses and telephone numbers of people or agencies who will listen and help such as Alcoholics Anonymous, the local Council on Alcoholism or a close friend.

In the end, it is the degree of commitment a problem drinker has to wanting to improve his life, combined with his frankness, determination and honesty which will help him achieve and maintain his drinking goal whether that is abstinence or controlled drinking.

Controlled drinking

In recent years it has been suggested that, for some drinkers, controlled drinking is an acceptable alternative to abstinence. However, before going on to discuss treatment which aims specifically at a controlled drinking goal, it is useful to know exactly what is meant by controlled drinking. It is not the same as social drinking.

Differences between controlled and social drinking

Social drinker	Controlled drinker
May buy 'rounds'	Avoids 'rounds'
May drink as and when he wants to	Plans drinking ahead
Drinks when appropriate	Each drink timed
Drinking pattern like that of contemporaries	Drinking pattern predetermined
Does not keep a record of drinking	Drinking self-monitored and recorded
May get drunk	May not get drunk

The social drinker can let his heart rule his drinking behaviour but the controlled drinker must use his head. Controlled drinking can be described as an acquired and complex skill like driving a car. At first, a learner driver has to concentrate on all aspects of the vehicle. Later, as his responses become more automatic, he is able to enjoy the experience. In the same way, a potential controlled drinker will need to concentrate on timing his drinks at first, planning a drinking pattern and keeping within pre-set limits. This may mean that he finds drinking is not very enjoyable at all to begin with. Later, however, controlled drinking can become second nature.

If harm-free drinking for many 'alcoholics' means total abstinence, how do you identify the few who will be able to be successful at controlled drinking? Some people have suggested that it is the 'mildly dependent alcoholic' who is most likely to benefit from this sort of treatment but that term is vague and it is probably best to try to set out definite reasons why someone should or should not be offered controlled drinking as a drinking goal. A lot of research remains to be carried out in this area but experience shows that certain characteristics seem to be important when offering people controlled drinking as a goal. These can be divided into first and second rank characteristics. People who do not have first rank characteristics would normally be considered unsuitable for controlled drinking. However, if they have second rank characteristics, it may be possible to consider them. It follows that the problem drinkers who are most likely to be successful with controlled drinking are those who have both first and second rank characteristics.

First rank characteristics
No permanent alcohol related physical damage
Living in a stable relationship
Relatively short drinking history

Second rank characteristics
No history of general compulsive behaviour
Alcohol not normally used to relieve tension
Evidence of moderate drinking in the past

If alcohol has produced physical damage, perhaps to the liver or the brain, it could well be suicidal to drink again, even in moderation. If the problem drinker is living in a stable relationship with a husband, wife, boyfriend, girlfriend, parent or someone who is concerned enough to help in the treatment programme, controlled drinking may be appropriate. It is not suitable for someone who is socially isolated or who lives in a lonely bedsitter. A short drinking history means that the 'alcoholic' has been drinking excessively for less than two or three years. This usually means, although not invariably, that controlled drinking is a more suitable approach for the younger 'alcoholic'. There are exceptions to this, such as Tom.

Tom

Tom is a man in his mid-50s who was referred to the Addiction Unit by his wife. She was beginning to worry about his drinking. He had been a modest drinker since being in the army in his youth. He had had a routine of visiting the pub on a Tuesday and Saturday but he never drank more than 3 pints. However, about a year ago, he was made redundant from a managerial job and since then he has had almost unlimited spare time and has felt somewhat depressed about being unemployed. He had some older, retired friends who met in the local club every lunchtime and evening. Tom began to join them. He was soon drinking 10 pints a day and bought a bottle of whisky every week. All this was quickly using up his redundancy money and for the first time he and his wife had begun to experience sexual and emotional difficulties.

Tom has the first rank characteristics. He has not yet developed any alcohol related illness, he has a caring wife and he has had a drink problem for only one year.

The second rank characteristics are less important but, nevertheless, ought to be considered when controlled drinking is being discussed as a treatment goal.

The treatment programme which is outlined next is a tentative set of guidelines for training in controlled drinking. Most of the treatment programmes for controlled drinking have been developed in the USA and are sometimes inappropriate for use in other countries. For example, drinking habits are different there and the traditional English pub does not exist. Because there is a large private sector, American hospitals can afford 'simulated bars' which NHS or local authority administrators would probably be quite reluctant to put at the top of the priority list for any hospital or unit. (Some of the other, more painful, psychological therapies such as aversion conditioning (associating electric shocks or nausea with drinking alcohol) have also been traditionally more popular in the USA than in Great Britain). The six steps to controlled drinking which we move on to discuss here have been adapted for use in this country and they have been used effectively in a number of cases, both in hospital and the community. Two treatment sessions a week seem to be about right.

Six steps to controlled drinking

These six steps to controlled drinking should be used in conjunction with the most appropriate steps from the section on harm-free drinking (see page 160) which are as important for the controlled drinker as they are for the abstainer. As an example, you might begin with Step 1 of harm-free drinking and go on to Steps 1 and 2 of controlled drinking. You could follow these with Steps 2 and 3 of harm-free drinking and so on, working out the best strategy for each individual case.

Six steps to controlled drinking – Checklist

Step 1   A period without drinking
Step 2   Teaching and training
Step 3   Learning how to drink
Step 4   Involving family and friends
Step 5   Long term aims
Step 6   Follow up

- **Step 1: A period without drinking**
  It does not seem unreasonable that any problem drinker who has committed himself to a goal of controlled drinking should begin by cutting out alcohol altogether for a period of time. Exactly how long this period should be varies from person to person but it seems unlikely that someone will become a successful controlled drinker if he cannot remain abstinent for at least some weeks or months. If there are any withdrawal symptoms, a period of abstinence is a must but it also helps an 'alcoholic's' confidence when he proves to himself that he can control his own drinking. However, because one of the features of alcohol dependence is a rapid return to heavy

drinking after abstinence, both the problem drinker and the person helping him need to monitor the return to drinking extremely carefully.

- **Step 2: Teaching and training**
  A period of abstinence can be used to teach the problem drinker about some of the effects of alcohol and about the principles of self-control.

Education about alcohol and its effect
Although some 'alcoholics', particularly those who have been in hospital, have acquired a detailed knowledge of alcohol and alcoholism, many people facing a drink problem know very little about the subject. 'The increase in alcoholism', 'Alcohol and the law', and 'The harm which alcohol causes' are all useful topics to discuss.

Many problem drinkers do not realise how strong various drinks can be. It is not unusual to hear the 'alcoholic' say, 'I have cut down to cider now' or, 'You cannot really be an "alcoholic" if you only drink beer'. He is quite surprised to learn that cider is often stronger than beer and that one pint of beer is equivalent to a double whisky. Other people are often astonished to find out how many middle-class 'alcoholics' there are. A short questionnaire which the problem drinker fills in before and after a teaching session can show roughly how much he has learned.

Teaching the principles of self-control
Learning self-control, in this context, means that a problem drinker learns how he can change the aspects of his behaviour which will have most influence on him being able to control the amount he drinks. In other words, a problem drinker is shown how, for example, re-arranging his day-to-day routine can affect how much he drinks.

The 'alcoholic' can be shown that excessive drinking is like many other behaviours in that it is influenced by circumstances and can produce consequences which are enjoyable in the short term but harmful in the long term. This means that escaping from problems by getting drunk can be pleasant immediately after drinking, but that next morning, things are much worse. Using examples like this, the 'alcoholic' can be shown how short term pleasure is a much more powerful influence on his behaviour than long term harm. He needs to change and to think in the long term.

This type of teaching may help the problem drinker to see that excessive drinking is not a disease but a behaviour which is affected by his emotions and environment. In short, the potential controlled drinker is taught that he can work at controlling his drinking.

- ### Step 3: Learning how to drink
  The 'alcoholic' not only drinks more than the social drinker but he also drinks in a completely different way.

Social drinker	'Alcoholic'
Usually mixes spirits	Often drinks spirits 'neat'
Sips rather than gulps	Takes large gulps
Drinks slowly	Drinks quickly
Drinks at same pace	Rushes the first two or three drinks
Rarely drinks before going out	Sometimes drinks before going out
Variable day to day drinking pattern	Stereotyped day to day drinking pattern

Perhaps the most striking difference is that the 'alcoholic' takes large gulps with a relatively long interval between each one. On the other hand, the social drinker takes more regular and more frequent, smaller sips. Overall, however, the 'alcoholic' drinks about three times faster.

The 'where' of drinking is just as important as the 'how'. Despite its importance in many of our lives, and in the lives of many 'alcoholics', the pub receives little attention in books about alcoholism. 'Alcoholics' are normally treated at home, in offices, consulting rooms or hospital wards, rarely in the pub. Yet, once the 'alcoholic' finishes active treatment, the pubs and their temptation will still be there. If someone is being trained in controlled drinking it would seem useful for part of his training to be carried out in a pub.

Despite the importance of the pub, a lot of excessive drinking goes on at home and this is potentially more dangerous because there are many aspects of the pub, not present in the home, which limit the amount an 'alcoholic' can drink such as price, conversation, friends and the landlord. Many drinkers of both sexes appreciate this and prefer not to drink at home at all during controlled drinking treatment. Because this is the case, this section will concentrate on social situations and particularly the pub. Until more research evidence is available, it is probably best to advise the controlled drinker not to drink at home, especially when he is alone.

As to what type of drink is best for controlled drinkers, it would seem best, again until further evidence is available, if spirits and fortified wines are banned in controlled drinking for two reasons.

1   With controlled drinking, there are rules about how much can be drunk. Beer and lager come in cans or glasses so that people know exactly how much they are drinking. On the other hand, when you start pouring your own spirits, it is difficult to know exactly how much is in a glass.
2   If someone follows a programme of controlled drinking, each drink has to last for a certain amount of time, but even with the best will in the world, it is not easy to make a pub measure of whisky last for half an hour. This timing is much more realistic if beer is the drink chosen.

Having discussed the 'how', 'where' and 'what' of controlled drinking, these three elements can be incorporated into the treatment plan which involves the person practising drinking in a controlled way, in a social setting and with the person who is helping him to act as a 'model drinker'. The problem drinker is shown how to sip drinks rather than gulp them, encouraged to set a time limit for each drink and to pace himself accordingly. He is told before he goes to the pub that he must have set a time for leaving and have decided how much he will drink. Training should ideally take place in different social settings and at different times of the day because one of the characteristics of 'alcoholics' is that they tend to drink in the same place and at the same time. The controlled drinker might be encouraged to talk about how he feels on these visits. Is he excited, depressed or tense? Can he cope with these emotions without feeling that he needs another drink? After a given number of drinks, he might also talk about how he feels now that he has had a couple of pints. The 'alcoholic' often drinks so quickly that he misses the pleasurable effects of just a few pints of beer.

174

Most people do not drink on every day of the week and so the potential controlled drinker should not have a drink on at least three days every week. It is relatively easy for him to keep to this when the person who is helping him is there to buy soft drinks, and so it might be useful if he also goes to the pub with other people who have not been involved in his treatment but who are aware of the problem. This simulates what might happen after active treatment has ended.

Exposure to temptation
It can be relatively easy for someone to control his drinking while he is being supervised but when he goes back to his normal routine he will invariably be under stress of some sort. It is quite possible that something particularly stressful would normally act as a cue for excessive drinking. A treatment programme should take this into account by exposing the controlled drinker to stress and helping him to continue controlled drinking afterwards. This happened with Bob.

Bob
Bob is a 33-year-old man who, despite undergoing all sorts of tests, was excessively worried about having a heart attack. His worries were temporarily forgotten after drinking heavily. For most of the time he remained in a chair at home and even after slight exertion he would be aware of his heart, would feel at risk and this would prompt him to drink. Bob's life consisted of sitting in his chair and drinking vast amounts of cider.

His stress experience during treatment consisted of taking increasingly vigorous exercise and counting his pulse rate before and after. When he had completed his jogging or skipping, he was accompanied to the pub for drinking skills practice. Initially, he found it extremely difficult to drink moderately but was eventually able to do so with encouragement. As he was exercising every day but was also required to be abstinent for three days every week, the exercise was followed by soft drinks on some occasions. As each session did not result in a heart attack, Bob felt increasingly less pressure to drink excessively.

Situations which tempt a person to drink excessively are different for everyone. They could include things like:

Chairing a meeting
Giving a talk

Going into a supermarket
Going to town
Visiting friends
Doing a task which is impossible to complete
Talking to someone of the opposite sex

It seems sensible that a comprehensive treatment programme should at least try to simulate some of the stress which a person may encounter in day-to-day life.

- ## *Step 4: Involving family and friends*
The wife or husband, parent, girlfriend or boyfriend of the problem drinker should be involved in treatment as much as possible. They should be encouraged to find out about the six steps to harm-free drinking and they should be told what controlled drinking is all about. Whenever possible, they should be offered leaflets and booklists on problem drinking. If an unhappy relationship is a major cause of drinking, marriage guidance or counselling with both partners may be appropriate. With the continued support and care of another person, the outlook for a problem drinker can be very much brighter. At some stage it might be a good idea to invite friends or children to a counselling session.

- ## *Step 5: Long term aims*
Long term drinking goals should be made as clear as possible. They can take the form of a contract which is negotiated by the helper, the controlled drinker and the wife or husband, partner or parent. It helps if the goals are realistic so that they do not lead to frustration. They will vary from person to person but it is surprising how similar they tend to be. The helper should be quite firm about the rules because he is more aware of potential pitfalls than the drinker. Once the rules have been drawn up, they can be typed on wallet sized cards for both patient and partner or parent. Tom (the man in an earlier example) has a controlled drinking card like the one shown on the next page.

Perhaps the most difficult question is what to do if things go wrong and the rules are broken. If rule breaking can be followed by something unpleasant, it will be less likely to happen. This could mean that the controlled drinker does not allow himself to indulge in activities which he normally enjoys such as smoking, watching television or reading for a fixed

```
The rules of my drinking
Drinking only after 8 pm except Sundays
No spirit/wine drinking. Beer/ordinary strength lager only
Three days' abstinence per week
4 pints per day maximum
16 pints per week absolute maximum
Avoid 'rounds'
At least half an hour per pint
Absolute honesty
```

period of time; the next week could be totally abstinent and the money normally spent on drink sent to an organisation of which the patient disapproves.

If the rules are broken on a number of occasions then the whole idea of controlled drinking must be reassessed and total abstinence considered.

- ### Step 6: Follow up
  After active treatment, there is follow up. Some helpers maintain regular contact with the people they have helped for up to two years. This seems to be about right in the case of the controlled drinker, with appointments each week at the beginning tailing off to monthly or bi-monthly visits if things are going well. The controlled drinker should keep a **personal drinking diary** in which he jots down information every day. The sort of information to include should cover the amount drunk, the time spent drinking, the situation (pub, club, etc), the mood before drinking and the mood after drinking.

  It can help if this record is discussed by the controlled drinker and his wife or whoever is close to him at a set time every week. Keeping a daily record in itself helps to stop people going back to old drinking habits. It can also be helpful if a note is kept of how much is spent each week on alcohol. Some controlled drinkers like to put aside part of the money they are saving by not drinking for a specific item such as a new coat, car or washing machine.

  It would seem unreasonable for somebody to be forced to remain a controlled, rather than a social, drinker for the rest of his life. Questions arise like:

  How long should the formal rules and record be maintained?
  Can a controlled drinker return to social drinking?
  Should drinking goals be eased as follow up progresses?

It is already well established that some 'alcoholics' vary between social drinking and problem drinking. From this, it might be assumed that even the successful controlled drinker will remain at risk to some degree. It has also been demonstrated that the longer someone abstains, the more likely he is to maintain abstinence. For example, the probability of cutting alcohol out completely is greater for someone who has abstained for a year than for someone who has abstained for only a month. However, whilst risk may be involved, it may be reasonable to suggest that, after a period of successful controlled drinking, the goals and record keeping could be stopped and social drinking could be attempted. Perhaps an intermediate stage of more relaxed controlled drinking would help to make an eventual return to social drinking.

In this chapter, an attempt has been made to outline a one-to-one approach to problem drinking. The section on harm-free drinking suggested exercises which, if carried out conscientiously, should help the 'alcoholic' to change his drinking habits. The section on controlled drinking is more speculative and it must be admitted that there are still respected people working in the field of alcohol dependence who feel that abstinence is the only realistic treatment goal. However, there is an increasing body of evidence which shows that some 'alcoholics' can moderate their drinking. It would seem short sighted if some interventions were not specifically designed to take this into account.

10 The group approach

Introduction

Individual treatment for 'alcoholics' as it was described in the previous chapter is relatively new to Great Britain. However, in this country, as in the USA, there is a tradition of group work as a way of dealing with alcoholism. Alcoholics Anonymous groups were among the very first interventions to be generally accepted as useful in combating alcoholism and group work is the basis of most of the activities in many Alcohol Treatment Units and Addiction Units.

There are many different opinions about the effectiveness of group work but there can be little doubt that the group experience is very powerful and can be a medium for change. However, group therapy need not be right in all cases and perhaps more attention should be given to matching problem drinkers to the most appropriate treatment, whatever it may be.

Stages in recovery

People who offer to help 'alcoholics' often blame themselves for the failure of group therapy. This is often counterproductive because the problem usually has nothing to do with the inadequacies of the staff. It is far more likely that they have not given sufficient thought to timing the changes they are helping the 'alcoholics' to make.

There seem to be four stages through which an 'alcoholic' must pass before he makes a final recovery (resolution) and, as each of these stages ends, there often seems to be a resistance on the part of the problem drinker to move on to the next stage and accept change.

If a helper wants to ensure that changes are made in the 'alcoholic's' way of life, it is important to be sensitive to this feeling of resistance and to make sure that it has been satisfactorily overcome before going on to the next stage.

Suggested stages in recovery

Conflict
Commitment

Bereavement
Rigid denial
Resolution

The first two stages of recovery, *conflict* and *commitment* have already been discussed in Chapter 9 (see page 161). Once an 'alcoholic' has decided to commit himself to treatment, an early part of the intervention will have to be abstinence, whatever results are hoped for eventually.

After the problem drinker has been abstinent for a week or so there may be some euphoria but it is more likely that there will be mood fluctuations and, increasingly, these will be of a depressive nature, perhaps a kind of *bereavement* reaction. The 'loss' of alcohol is a very serious one to the 'alcoholic' and it is at this stage that further progress is sometimes blocked. In this case, the 'alcoholic' will resist by using his favourite psychological defence of denial. To change life any more than he has already is far too threatening a prospect and so the problem drinker vigorously *denies* any further problems of a psychological nature, 'I've stopped drinking, what more do you want me to do?' It is often clear that many people merely exist with abstinence and that they really do need more help to readjust to life without drink. If the *denial* of other problems, the third stage of resistance, can be overcome, then the 'alcoholic' is on the home straight and heading for recovery and the *resolution* of his problem.

Should we start a group?

Some advantages of group work

It is a potential medium for change
It can be a compelling experience in itself
It offers hope
It is conducive to making emotional links
The 'alcoholic' has people to copy social skills from
There may be social activities outside the group
There is support outside the group
It is an economical use of helpers' time

Being part of any therapy group seems to be a very powerful experience and it is possible to see significant change, even in groups which have no very definite aims. If a problem drinker attends a group regularly, it often indicates that there will probably be positive results from treatment and, in fact, for many patients who have become socially isolated, the group is the most important event of their week and seems to benefit even those members who rarely participate.

Helpers vary in their views about activities which happen outside the group sessions. However, it is probably best to allow people to exchange addresses and telephone numbers if they want to, though women should be cautioned about offering their addresses to men who, in the group, appear pleasant and interesting but who could be unwelcome visitors in the middle of the night if they were drunk. In general, however, social activities outside the group setting are beneficial. After all, it is very hard to find a social scene where there is no temptation to drink. Members of a group can be very supportive to one another when 'slip-ups' occur and they will often help each other out, perhaps by staying with someone who has started drinking and sobering him up or by getting him to hospital.

It has often been said that a major advantage of group work is that more people can be seen in a given time. This is only partly true because a lot of time has to be spent writing down what happened at each session and sometimes individuals need to be seen outside group time. It is very important to monitor progress and to watch closely for members of the group who may need individual help.

What kind of group?

Checklist

General groups
Support group
Educational group
Psychotherapy group
Skills group *etc*

Special groups
Women's group
Adolescents' group
Wives' group
Occupational group *etc*

• General groups

Support group

A support group is particularly suitable for people who are stuck at the 'bereavement' or 'denial' phases of recovery as described on page 181. Alcoholics Anonymous groups are good examples of support groups. They are totally non-threatening, everyone is welcomed, tea or coffee is available and there is no pressure to take part. The group enjoys talking about past drinking exploits and yet the members also know that sobriety has been vital in achieving and maintaining the good aspects of life as they exist now. Support groups are a place of comfort in times of trouble (and not just trouble caused by drink: an overdose or some other cry for help can be avoided when there is a safe and supportive place to bring a problem). Although change, such as that from drunkenness to sobriety, does occur in support groups, nobody needs to have a personal goal to aim at. The work of the group is usually more concerned with discussing whatever problems or crises are worrying group members in any particular session.

Educational group

An educational group is much more structured than other groups and this sort of structure can bridge the gap between intensive treatment and rather looser aftercare such as the support group. One appeal of this kind of group is that it is not over-demanding on staff because different people can lead sessions on different topics, although it is probably important to have one helper who is present at all the sessions and can give a sense of caring and continuity. Subjects for sessions include such topics as anxiety management, self-control techniques, aspects of alcohol related harm and facilities available for problem drinkers.

Psychotherapy group

Although a psychotherapy group may be valuable at any stage in treatment, it is often best if it is the treatment chosen for patients who have achieved abstinence and are not too threatened at the prospect of finding a way out of the psychological maze they feel trapped in. This kind of psychotherapy group will be particularly concerned with looking at personal interactions and the group's goals will be about sorting out emotions. Anger, depression and animosity will need to find new and appropriate methods of expression; and trust, a sense of belonging and a sense of caring for others will need to be rediscovered. There will be a conscious move to discuss drinking as little as possible and to deal with crises only briefly, at least in the group. However, it is possible to use the reaction and behaviour of someone in the group who is faced with a crisis as a stimulus for group discussion. A psychotherapy group of this kind should not exceed 10 members, new members should be introduced only at well spaced intervals and the group should expect to stay together for 10–18 months.

Social skills group
This type of group normally has quite specific aims. Social skills are really those aspects of behaviour which we use when talking to or interacting with other people. Such skills can include basic needs like voice projection, posture, eye contact and gesticulation. At a better level they can involve the when, what and how of interaction with others. Most of us take such skills for granted although they are learned rather than innate. A social skills group can be beneficial for those people who feel ill at ease, anxious, or embarrassed in company and the aim of such a group is to teach people the appropriate skills to use in a certain setting. Group members often practise these behaviours in pairs and then the group as a whole discusses how well they did. Homework can involve practising the skills in real life situations and bringing a record of what happened to the next group meeting. These groups are run for a specific number of sessions, perhaps about 10 and each session is devoted to some particular aspect of social behaviour.

- **Special groups**
Special groups may be run in any way that seems appropriate. For example, a women's group could be a support group or a social skills group.
  There are two reasons to consider setting up special groups. The first reason is that there is much more likely to be trust, togetherness and sharing of feelings when all the members have something in common besides a drink problem. This might be homosexuality or wishing to talk about menstrual difficulties. It is much easier to respect confidentiality in a special group. This is quite important for people such as doctors or publicans who might find it difficult being in the same

group as a patient or customer. The second reason is that the other feature which group members have in common, apart from drinking, may be central to their lives and yet be something that would rarely be touched on in an unselected group. For example, if a skid row 'alcoholic' or a young adult needed help, the problems of skid row or adolescence would receive scant attention in an unselected group.

Setting up a group

Group work can make a lot of demands on helpers' time, not least because sessions are often held outside office hours. It can be such an emotional drain that the advice must be to think carefully before setting up a group and to prepare for it thoroughly.

Points to consider before starting a group

Who is it for?
Who will be excluded?
What are the aims?
Who will be co-helper?
Do the helpers agree on their roles in the group?
Where will sessions be held?
When will sessions be held?
How long will the sessions be?
Will the group be open or closed?
What will be the life-span of the group?
What will the group rules be?
What preparation is needed?
What problems can be anticipated?

To be certain that your thoughts are quite clear it may help to write details of the proposed group down on paper and to discuss them with colleagues or the team that you work with.

Who the group is for is usually determined by a particular need or interest but it may be important to think about who the group is not for. A common difficulty is that problem drinkers often attend a variety of groups which all have different aims. This may result in terrible confusion, for example, when someone who attends an Alcoholics Anonymous group which tries to maintain abstinence in an atmosphere of warmth and support also belongs to a psychotherapy group with its much more threatening atmosphere.

The choice of a co-helper is crucial because you may be working together for up to two years. You need to agree on all aspects of the group and particularly on how you see each other's role in the group. Husband and wife teams often make good group leaders but there are no fixed rules about what the backgrounds of the helpers should be.

Fixing the time and place for sessions may seem trivial but they can be important factors. The place should be easily accessible and not in a part of town notorious for muggings. If the sessions are held in a large centre it may help to put up signs for the first week or two, to show members the way to the room. The time is probably less important but it would be silly to hold a wives' group when some prospective members will be picking up their children from school.

It is up to the helpers to decide who should belong to the group. All the prospective members should know what the aims of the group are, how long the group will run, how often they are expected to attend, and what expectations there are. Will it be possible to see helpers outside the group setting? Are group members allowed to seek additional help from other agencies? What will happen if they leave the group? These are all questions which should be answered. If the assessment meeting is not held where the group will normally meet, it is important to give clear instructions as to the best way to get to the regular meeting place.

Confidentiality is always a big issue for problem drinkers and the helpers must make their own professional commitment to confidentiality clear and they must be emphatic that the same confidentiality is expected from anybody who joins the group. It is wise to expect problems and to have contingency plans ready. Non-attendance and high drop-out rates bedevil groups which are set up for 'alcoholics', but once members become attached to a group they are likely to stay with it and they will eventually do well. One of the advantages of running an open group, where new members keep joining and others leave, is that you only have to get the group off the ground once. Another way to minimise drop-out is to circulate a summary of each session to all the group members so that if anyone does miss a session he will be kept in touch with what has happened. Members who arrive intoxicated can also frustrate a group and the session will be dominated by the drinker. As the group becomes more self-assured it will add to the rules laid down by the helper and the group should be pushed at an early stage to decide what should be done if a member arrives drunk.

Monitoring the group

It is extremely difficult to evaluate how effective group work is and it is equally hard to determine how to decide what is success for someone who has a drink problem. It is not enough to look at how much alcohol a group member drinks because his overall quality of life may improve even when his drinking is getting worse. It is worthwhile trying to decide how success and failure will be measured before starting a group. It is also interesting and important to monitor what is going on in the group session by session. The group process rating scale is a quick way of doing this.

Group process rating scale

Non-assertive	1 2 3 4 5 6 7 8 9 10	Assertive
Insensitive to others' feelings	1 2 3 4 5 6 7 8 9 10	Sensitive to others' feelings
Fails to use group learning	1 2 3 4 5 6 7 8 9 10	Uses group learning
Non-participating in group process	1 2 3 4 5 6 7 8 9 10	Participating in group process
Pessimistic of success in therapy	1 2 3 4 5 6 7 8 9 10	Optimistic of success in therapy

After each session every member of the group is rated 1 to 10 in each of the five dimensions of the group process rating scale. Each dimension is defined as follows:

Assertive: Expresses his feelings and opinions confidently. Does not change his opinion readily when challenged. Uses positive statements when talking about his attitudes.

Sensitive: Responsive to other people. Tends to recognise others' difficulties and to help them through sticky patches.

Uses group learning: Applies the new knowledge and skills he has learned about through group experiences.

Participating in group process: Engages in verbal and non-verbal group activities but not necessarily in an initiating role.

Optimistic of success in therapy: Inclined to take realistic favourable views about the value of therapy when there are suitable grounds for hope.

Ideally, each helper should rate each session independently. Monitoring the group in this way should make the helpers more aware of what is going on in their group and should make it easier to evaluate the group later.

Many problem drinkers find it extremely difficult to talk openly about their feelings and to get along with other people. It is in helping 'alcoholics' to overcome these difficulties together that group work has found its strengths and, despite the advances which have been made in group work theory and practice over the years, that is as true today as it was when the very first groups of Alcoholics Anonymous began to meet.

11 Measuring recovery

Introduction

Success in treating alcoholism depends on what you mean by success. Is it possible to say that someone whose treatment goal was abstinence is a success if he no longer drinks but continues to be aggressive towards his family? In the same way, can someone who still drinks heavily even after treatment, but whose general ability to cope with life has improved, be called a failure? Success in treatment is notoriously difficult to measure objectively.

What makes a recovery successful?

Although it is very difficult to work out how effective treatment has been, it is not good enough just to assume that more treatment must automatically be better than less. Some attempt, however inadequate, must be made to evaluate treatment and a number of issues need to be borne in mind:

Why assess the outcome of treatment?

How many 'alcoholics' get better without any treatment?

What kind of person is being treated?

What criteria are to be used to measure successful treatment?

When is a good time to assess how successful treatment has been?

There are two broad reasons for trying to assess outcome. Firstly, there are harsh critics who argue that any treatment for 'alcoholics' is a waste of time and that it would be better to divert scarce resources to the treatment of other conditions where the chance of success is better. Getting money for a project is always difficult and will certainly be a non-starter if there is no data to suggest that it may be beneficial. Secondly, it is a matter of self-discipline to look at your own work to see if there are ways of improving. Sometimes, it is necessary to ask yourself whether your work is really worthwhile or whether you are just doing it because you like doing it. There is nothing wrong with finding that a particular method does not work too well (even if it was your own idea!) and changing your approach. The danger is in becoming complacent and reluctant to change.

All the indications are that somewhere between 5% and 15% of people who would be labelled problem drinkers recover spontaneously without ever seeking help and return to social drinking. In fact, recovery is probably not really spontaneous at all but happens after some important change in someone's life such as a move to a new job, getting married or experiencing a religious conversion.

Evidence suggests that if someone is treated for alcoholism, there is a much better chance of recovery than if there is no intervention. The actual type of treatment does not seem to matter too much and even a single counselling session can be expected to result in an improvement in about half of all cases whilst, with more intensive treatment, up to three-quarters of patients will improve. Some of the most imaginative research into outcome has been undertaken by an American alcohol specialist, Raymond M. Costello, who has made an in-depth review of most of the published work relating to the results of treatment. He found, very broadly speaking, that good results were associated with:

Patients who had a stable background, both social and psychological.

Active and intensive treatment, whatever it may be.

A sense of sharing and participating in a community during treatment.

Working with a patient's relatives, colleagues and friends as well as with the patient himself.

The use of *Antabuse* and *Abstem* (though see page 49).

Effective follow up after the initial treatment had finished.

The person who is most likely to recover well from a drink problem will be in a fairly stable social position. If he has a job and is married, the outlook is relatively good, even without treatment. But there are pitfalls here. Some jobs are in high risk occupations (see Chapter 4) and not all marriages are equally stable. Good signs to look for in a marriage are when household work is shared, when feelings are shared and when the 'non-alcoholic' partner has not been badly neglected and abused because of drinking.

As for a drinking pattern which might indicate that a successful outcome is possible, periods of abstinence or controlled drinking of more than six months and a short total period of problem drinking are good signs. Another good sign is when the cause of the problem drinking is something obvious and easily remedied. Bad signs for successful recovery are when someone drinks to relieve unpleasant feelings such as depression, anxiety and inadequacy, and tends to act on impulse.

It is often said that an 'alcoholic' needs to be motivated if he is to do well and it is true that someone who is well motivated will do better than someone who is not. However, it is also true that most problem drinkers who come forward for treatment are in conflict: they want to stop drinking and yet, at the same time, they still want to carry on (see Chapter 9). Part of treatment is to resolve this conflict and to help them to want to do something about the problem drinking. If an 'alcoholic' has determined that he wants to stop drinking when intervention begins, your job is already half done!

Measuring success will probably be different for each case which you deal with. Every 'alcoholic' has different problems in the first place and will want to achieve his own special aims in treatment. It is helpful to talk these aims over with the problem drinker before treatment begins and to make them as specific as possible. However, these tailor-made aims will nearly always fall into general categories which will help you to make as objective an assessment of success as possible. The categories are:

Success Checklist

Achieved and maintained drinking goal	Abstinence or controlled drinking
Reduced harm	Physical, psychological and social harm
Less time in institutions	Hospital and prison
Improved integration	Family and relationships
Improved social performance	Work and finances

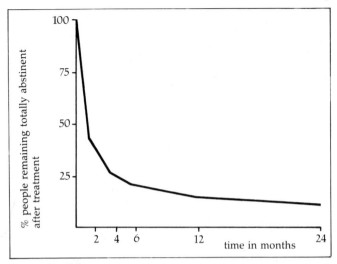

Figure 15: Relapse curve

It is almost as difficult to decide when you should try to judge success as it is to decide what success itself is. However, most alcohol specialists now agree that six months after presenting for treatment is the key time for a problem drinker. If he is going to fail, he will probably have failed or relapsed by this time. Figure 15 shows how the failure rate evens out after these first six months.

Improving intervention

It is now generally accepted that detecting problem drinking earlier means a better chance of successful treatment. This has implications for training in many areas such as medicine, social work, the probation service, teaching and the ministry. Everyone training for these professions needs to be aware of the effects of alcohol, to know how to identify and help a problem drinker and to know what specialist services are available. Workers in these professions must also be encouraged to take on the more straightforward cases of problem drinking and to select the cases which they refer to specialist agencies with care.

Many problem drinkers are reluctant to be referred on, because it means that they are seen as 'alcoholics' and they prefer to be helped by someone they know and trust such as their GP or social worker. For their part, alcohol specialists will have to be prepared to accept the more difficult cases and to offer active support and education to all primary workers (see Chapter 13).

Preventing problems in the first place

The numbers of people who drink either very heavily or, at the other end of the scale, not at all, are very similar to those people who either overindulge in or abstain from many other social activities, such as having sex or eating out. A minority group abstains, most people indulge in moderation and a small number is totally obsessed. This distribution can best be understood as a graph (Figure 16).

The graph is called the Ledermann curve, after the French epidemiologist who first described this theory. It is important to note that, whilst about 7% of the population of Great Britain do not drink at all, an even smaller number of people drink more than the 100 grams a day danger limit.

It is also interesting to see what happens if the total amount of alcohol drunk in the country increases. (Records kept by the Customs and Excise Department show the total amount drunk in the country each year and from this figure it is possible to work out the *per capita* consumption, the amount each adult drinks in a year). There are several possibilities.

The number of people who do not drink could have fallen.

The whole of the increase could be accounted for by heavy drinkers drinking more.

Everybody who drinks could be drinking a little more.

There is good research evidence to suggest that when there is an increase in the total amount of alcohol drunk, that is, an increase in *per capita* consumption, it is the third possibility that operates; namely, everyone who drinks is drinking a little more. This suggests that many more people may find themselves at risk of being beyond the 100 grams a day line and of

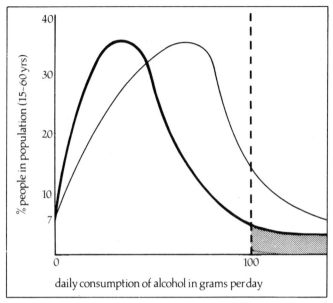

Figure 16: Ledermann curve

being problem drinkers. The lighter line in Figure 16 illustrates what happens when *per capita* consumption increases. If, on the other hand, total alcohol consumption goes down, the reverse happens.

There are implications here for preventing all sorts of problems associated with drinking. By raising prices, making licensing hours shorter and a whole range of other measures, the Government has the ability to reduce the country's total alcohol consumption and so to lower the number of people at risk from alcohol related problems. Many of us would argue that radical steps such as closing pubs at lunch time or increasing the real price of spirits sharply may well be the most effective strategy to deal with alcoholism. The counter argument is to ask why the vast majority of people should be inconvenienced or deprived of their lunch time drink, their evening out or their whisky nightcap because of a relatively small number of problem drinkers.

Improved alcohol education causes no-one any hardship and can be an effective way of preventing an increase in problem drinking. There have been a number of national and regional campaigns aimed at increasing the general public's awareness of the effects of alcohol. There have also been campaigns aimed at cutting down the number of incidents of drinking and driving. Films about the dangers of alcohol are available either free or on hire and many specialist alcohol agencies and Health Education offices can supply posters and leaflets from a variety of sources.

More and more attention is also being paid, particularly by Alcohol Advice Centres and local health education officers, to the need to educate children, young people and adults about the dangers, as well as the pleasures, of alcohol. No-one is too young or too old to learn. It is worth noting that most health education officers and staff at Alcohol Advice Centres are happy to be invited to come along to a school, youth club or anywhere a group meets.

However, anyone who tries to mount a campaign aimed at preventing problem drinking will probably face any combination of four unseen pressures:

The great majority of the population of Great Britain approves of drinking.

State, industry and trade all benefit when alcohol consumption increases or is maintained.

Alcohol, in moderation, does have beneficial effects.

In general, harm from drinking is seen as a distant and remote possibility.

It is difficult to say just how effective alcohol education and associated advertising campaigns are. No-one can know how many more people would have risked drinking and driving if they had not seen one of the advertisements or heard one of the warnings and the results of some educational projects may not be apparent for years, until the children who took part in them begin drinking.

The signs are that campaigns and education may make moderate drinkers more moderate. If this is true, it should mean that fewer people reach the 100 grams a day mark shown in Figure 16. As for the problem drinker, it seems that he is immune to any amount of warnings about the dangers of drink. As usual, he is the last one to admit that he has any problem.

12 Working with young people

Introduction

At a Health Education exhibition held in Leeds, groups of junior school children were encouraged to talk freely about alcohol. In any group, there was rarely more than one child who could not name at least three or four different alcoholic drinks. Later in the discussions, it emerged that most of them had tasted some alcoholic drink in the previous few months. They knew the most appropriate drinks for various occasions such as Christmas, birthdays and weddings, they knew what effect drinking had on the way their parents behaved and one enthusiastic nine-year-old even claimed that he knew how it felt to be drunk (to his teacher's horror!).

The children of 20 years ago would have known a lot less about alcohol at that age and only a few of them would ever have tasted alcohol while still at junior school. Some people may say that all this talk of drink is a product of the permissive society whilst others may argue that it is due to a more open attitude to education.

Whatever the reason, the fact remains that children are becoming aware of the existence of alcoholic drinks at an early age. This means that there is a need to make them aware from the age of five of the possible dangers, as well as the pleasures, of the drinking that most of them will be doing by the time they reach the age of 15.

Education and drinking in adolescence will be discussed later in this chapter but, first of all, the question must be asked, how do young children learn about alcohol in their early years?

Learning about drinking

- ## Learning from parents' drinking

Normal families Checklist

Children mimic parents' behaviour

Children are acutely aware of what is happening
around them

Example of parents

Parents must answer questions honestly

Many children watch their parents enjoying a drink with
friends and are sometimes invited to join in the fun with a
soft drink of their own. This not only happens at home but
also on family treats at a pub in the country which has a
pleasant garden, or at the local sports club when the whole
family celebrates dad's win. Some of these children may well
have tasted an alcoholic drink either as a treat or as a regular
part of their lemonade shandy.

Children as young as two or three mimic adult behaviour
and a toddler drinking orange juice may well shout out with
a broad grin, 'I'm drinking beer!' Children are always acutely
aware of what is happening around them and an enquiring
child will always want to do what mummy and daddy are
doing. Hopefully, the parents will be able to show by their
own example and teaching that there are pleasant aspects to
drinking when alcohol is used sensibly.

Parents should always be prepared to answer their children's questions about alcohol and drinking honestly. If a
child is told that it is none of his business it will only make
him more inquisitive and eager to find out for himself what
is so magical and mysterious about this drink which he is not
allowed to enjoy.

Alcohol in the wrong hands can be extremely dangerous
and several cases of alcohol poisoning in young people between 3 and 14 have been reported. The children have come
downstairs on the morning after a party at home when their
parents have been too tired or too drunk to bother clearing
up. No child can resist the temptation to eat and drink some
of the party leftovers, sometimes with disastrous results.
Blood alcohol levels in some children have been found to be
as high as 200 mg%, a dangerously high level of intoxication.
Usually, if the children are taken to hospital fairly quickly, no
harm is done; but there is the danger of alcohol poisoning,
especially when mum and dad are still dead to the world and
even a crying child cannot rouse them.

- *Learning from parents' drinking in an 'alcoholic' family* (see also Chapter 3)

'Alcoholic' families Checklist

Little contact with friends and grandparents, aunts and uncles

Heavy drinking seen as normal

No family activities with the 'alcoholic' parent

Some children deprived of food, toys, books, holidays

Children feel inferior

Children avoid contact with 'alcoholic' parent

Children suffer violence

Some children are quite seriously affected by the consequences of their parents' drinking. They can suffer deprivation and, in some cases, quite serious harm.

Social deprivation
The children of 'alcoholics' are often denied opportunities that normal families take for granted. They may not be given the chance to develop friendships and they may miss out on the support of other members of their family such as grandparents and aunts and uncles because either one or both of their parents is preoccupied with drinking. Their only social contact is likely to be with other families where the parents drink heavily, and they are likely to gain the impression that heavy drinking is quite normal.

Material deprivation
Drinking is a very costly activity and, in some families, this may mean that the children cannot have adequate nutrition or regular meals. They are poorly clothed and are not able to have the same toys, books and holidays as the children of normal families.

However, in some families where there is a drinking problem but where money is no object, heavy drinking parents may try to buy their children off by giving them extravagant presents and vast amounts of pocket money. These are a poor substitute for love and warmth of feeling.

Emotional deprivation
Drinking can have such an effect on the relationship between parents and children that feelings towards the drinking parent may become ambivalent or even totally negative. Mood changes associated with heavy drinking, from misery to aggression to sickening pleasantness, may confuse a child so much in his relationship with a heavy drinking parent that he avoids contact completely.

What happens next is that the child may form an abnormal attachment to his 'non-alcoholic' parent, which in its turn may influence the way he sees his parents' roles in the family.

Physical harm
About 60% of non-accidental injuries to children may be caused directly or indirectly by alcohol abuse. What often happens is that when a problem drinker has been too intoxicated to cope with demanding children or a crying baby, aggression has seemed the only solution.

Injury caused by negligence in families where there is a problem drinker can also be common. It has even been known for a baby to be suffocated when his mother fell into a drunken sleep with him in her arms.

Psychological harm
Whilst some children are naturally resilient and can learn to cope with a heavy drinking parent, others need treatment for problems which they develop such as:

Bed wetting
Truancy
Petty crime
Speech impediments

● ***Learning from the media***
Many scenes in radio and television programmes take place in the bar of the pub or hotel where everybody is having a drink and enjoying himself. It sometimes seems that the first

thing anybody does when he arrives home is to have a drink. Friends call round and out comes the bottle again. A celebration? Time for a drink. Depressed? Have a drink. Nobody ever seems to refuse a drink because he is driving; nobody ever seems to prefer a soft drink.

Children are acutely aware of what goes on around them (even after 9 pm when the media imagine they are tucked up in bed) and it could well be that television in particular influences their attitude towards alcohol.

- ***Learning from advertising***
  Many children and young people see alcoholic drinks advertised on TV, on the cinema screens, on hoardings and in the press. They must be influenced by advertising. If not, why would products specifically designed for young people be advertised at all?

  Some experts have suggested that limiting or banning alcohol advertising may be one way of preventing some problem drinking. However, the issue is a sensitive one and the right to advertise is hotly defended by the various drinks industries.

Drinking among young people

The highest number of drunkenness convictions for all age groups is for young adults of 18. This can be partly explained by the fact that 18 is the age when young people are first allowed to drink in public houses legally. Drinkers of this age are often not used to drinking heavily. Eighteenth birthday celebrations may become a little boisterous and when this happens the police may be called in. However, in many cases, a first offence is the last.

What is more disturbing is the number of drunkenness offences committed by young people under the age of 18, mostly at the ages of 16 and 17 but, in some cases, even lower. This trend may mean that young people really do look older than they are. This, in its turn, makes it more difficult to detect under-age drinkers and to enforce the licensing laws. Some people suggest that better control of 'off-sales' (which may be where most young people who drink under-age buy their alcohol) might improve matters. However, this is questionable because the drink is often bought by someone in a group of friends who is either 18 or looks that age.

It must be remembered that at 16, young people may be almost mature physically, but they are still in a crucial stage of their emotional development and may not have matured psychologically. Some cases coming before the courts now include people whose psychological development has been impaired by heavy drinking from an early age. Problem drinkers in their twenties and thirties who attend Alcohol Advice Centres and Treatment Units may well have psychological problems and most of them have often begun drinking at the age of 13 or 14.

There are many reasons why young people drink and some of them are the same as for any other drinker: alcoholic drinks have a pleasant taste, they change moods and, in moderation, they decrease inhibitions and relieve tension. Another reason may be that alcohol is widely available in an increasing number of supermarkets, local shops and off-licences where it seems that licensing laws may be less stringently enforced. There has been a general increase in alcohol consumption over the years and young people are as likely to be affected by an increase in consumption as anyone else.

In many areas there are very few places for young people to meet and the pub is warm and comfortable. Some of the entertainment available, such as video games, fruit machines, juke boxes and discos may make them especially attractive to young people. Even though some young people may not drink alcohol when they first go to pubs (it is legal for them to go into pubs from the age of 14), the atmosphere is likely to encourage them to want to drink, particularly when they are part of a group and there is pressure to conform.

Possible reasons why young people drink – Checklist

Wide availability of alcoholic drinks. (Many supermarkets and other shops have begun to sell alcoholic drinks and the number of off-licences has increased.)

General increase in alcohol consumption

Licensing laws not enforced stringently

Nothing else to do in the area except to go to the pub

Pressures from friends

The mood-changing effects of alcohol

Parents are not sufficiently aware and vigilant

Drinking habits modelled on those of parents

Drinking is the grown-up thing to do

Drinking to excess is a form of adolescent rebellion

There is a mystery about pubs and drinking which intrigues young people

---

Whilst research indicates that a large proportion of young adults who drink do so fairly moderately and responsibly, and enjoy the pleasant effects of alcohol, there is a minority who regularly drink too much at parties, in pubs, in parks and on street corners. This group is the cause for concern and, unfortunately, it also seems to be the focus for the attention of the media. This small number of young people makes sure that all young people have a bad name. They are the ones who regularly come to the notice of youth workers, police, social workers and teachers because:

● They commit offences when they are drunk such as drunkenness, assault and theft.

● They are caught drinking under-age in public houses.

● They are involved in a drinking and driving incident when they are driving with more than the legal 80 mg% limit of alcohol in their blood.

● They cause trouble at youth clubs and discos.

● There is a decline in school performance and they fail to complete assignments, are often absent from school and go drinking at lunchtimes returning to school smelling of drink.

● They are found drinking in such places as the local park or in the vicinity of a youth club.

Parents may suspect that their teenage sons and daughters have been drinking excessively if:

- There are repeated requests for extra money.
- The son or daughter comes in and goes straight to bed.
- There are incidents of bed wetting.
- There are early morning headaches and sickness.

It is important to remember that young people often experiment with alcohol because they discover that it can change their mood. However, experimentation can often get carried away and if a young person comes into a youth club or comes home behaving very strangely, smelling of drink and is obviously drunk, it could well be worth calling an ambulance in case they have drunk a fatal dose of alcohol. One young Liverpool girl managed to drink 2 pints of beer and a whole bottle of vermouth on her first drinking session before she realised that something was not quite right and staggered into the youth club! In fact, cases like this may often indicate that there is some sort of personal or family problem which needs sympathetic understanding. It is probably best not to turn a drunk young person out onto the street where he is at risk but to put him into a room where he can sober up.

If you do come across a young person who is drinking excessively and having problems, it is important not to be condemning. Young people are often sensitive and feel guilty about their drinking. They may be attempting to identify with adult behaviour or responding to pressure from their friends. Many young people are unaware of exactly how strong the various drinks are and find it difficult to cope with the effect it has on the way they behave.

How you react will vary according to the circumstances which bring a young person's drinking to your notice. It is important to discuss the topic (possibly together with parents) and to ensure that the young person is aware of the effects which alcohol can have.

It often happens that the young person you help to understand about drinking is a member of group of friends who all drink and a better way of dealing with the problem might be to talk things over with the whole group. It may well turn out that drinking is only a secondary issue and that the real problem is all about how the member of the group who drinks heavily sees himself, and about how he sees his status and role within the group. He is often merely trying to live up to the expectations of his friends. Sorting out these problems can also help to sort out the drink problem. Dealing with a group of young people who have all drunk too much and are rowdy and aggressive is difficult. If all else fails, you should call in the police.

Alcohol education

It is because children are aware from the age of five or six (or even earlier) of alcoholic drinks and because young people often have their first drink between ten and twelve that good alcohol education is vital as early as possible if they are to grow up to enjoy drinking moderately, responsibly and without developing problems. Young people need to be aware of how alcohol affects them and of the problems it can cause.

- ### What needs to be taught about alcohol?
  If you are involved in teaching young people about alcohol in school, in a youth club or in any other setting, the objectives of the teaching remain the same. They are to:

Increase knowledge about alcoholic drinks.

Increase awareness of the effects of alcohol on the body and mind.

Understand the behaviour associated with drinking.

Examine society's attitudes towards drinking.

Understand the pressures friends can exert.

Explore the situations which may develop involving drink.

Be aware of the skills needed to make decisions about drinking.

Promote responsible drinking.

Your local Health Education Officer, Council on Alcoholism or TACADE (see Appendix 1) should be able to provide you with a list of teaching materials such as posters, leaflets, films and tape/slide presentations.

- ***Teaching about alcohol in schools***

Primary school
Perhaps the best lessons in which to begin teaching about alcoholic drinks are those which include teaching about the things we eat and drink. Pupils can be encouraged to bring pictures of drinks which are commonly used to school and the pictures could be grouped together under the headings such as:

Drinks children like

Drinks adults like

Drinks both children and adults like

Drinks which help to feed us

Drinks which children are not allowed

In this way, children can get to know about the effects of alcoholic drinks and the names of some of them.

Middle school
At the middle school level, more detailed information about alcohol could be included in:

Chemistry	Properties of alcohol Types of alcohol Production methods Fermentation and distillation Industrial and household uses
Biology	Consumption, absorption and the action of alcohol on the organs of the body Effects on the central nervous system
General science/ hygiene	Health aspects Alcohol as a food and its nutritional value The varying strengths of different drinks Blood alcohol levels Accidents caused by drinking too much alcohol
Social studies	Use of alcohol for socialisation The relationship of alcohol and crime Effects on behaviour The problems alcohol can cause in families

	Examination of social attitudes and pressures from friends
	Traditional customs such as buying rounds and using alcohol at celebrations
Geography	Areas of production
	Grain, grape and special ingredients
	Industrial and agricultural influences
History	Use of alcohol in the past
	Discovery of alcohol
	Ancient methods of production
	Patterns of consumption
	Development of traditions and customs
	Development of laws
	Temperance movements
Economics	Fiscal controls
	Effects of price on demand
	Contribution made by alcohol to the economy
	The part played by alcohol in exports and employment
Religious/ moral education	Reference to alcohol in the Old and New Testaments
	Religions such as Islam and denominations of Christianity such as the Salvation Army and the Baptists which forbid alcohol
	Effects on relationships and decision making
	Moral issues
	Advertising

High/senior school

At this stage, pupils will often find themselves being offered a drink at home, in clubs and restaurants, and at parties (see Appendix 4). As well as going over some of the factual aspects again, there might also be opportunities to look at ideas on drinking and to deal with problems. It can be useful to examine situations where pupils have been faced with pressure from their friends to drink.

It is important to consider the health aspects of drinking in more detail and for pupils to be aware of what alcohol dependence is (see Chapters 1 and 2). Knowing where they can find advice and help is also useful and information on what is available locally can often be provided by a local Council on

Alcoholism. (The staff of the council will probably be happy to come and speak.)

There is room at this stage for 'experimental' learning and pupils could be encouraged to find out things for themselves by undertaking project work in small groups. Films and discussion groups might also be useful ways of getting young people to talk about their attitudes and problems.

Pastoral care

In some schools, certain teachers have a specialist responsibility for pastoral care and they are in a position to help pupils who are at risk from their problem drinking. Care should be taken to find out about pupils who are affected by problem drinking in the family (see Chapter 3). When a pupil's attendance or academic performance falls off it is worth suspecting that a drink problem (either his own or in his family) may be the cause.

- ### Teaching about alcohol in youth groups

  Alcohol education in youth groups, where members are not forced to attend, must be attractively presented. If someone comes along to give an hour long lecture, he might well find himself without an audience after the first few minutes. As with High School groups, project work can be interesting but one idea for a club where there are other attractions is to set a film going in a separate room and to let people come and go as they please, choosing whether or not they want to watch it. It is something which can be done with different films on a variety of aspects of alcohol education (and other subjects) over a period of time.

  If you decide that this might work with your group, it is also worth keeping bright alcohol education posters pinned up which might stimulate discussion. Another point which should be borne in mind is that a leader should make it known that he is always available to talk about anything to do with alcohol. He should make sure that he is well-informed and that he can easily find the time to sit and talk about the problems that will almost inevitably come up.

Alcohol education is an important part of health education and requires skilful and well planned teaching. Asking someone to come in to speak about alcoholism to the final year in their last term or to the 18-year-olds in the youth club is probably completely worthless because attitudes will already have been formed and many young people will not take such a talk seriously. They will often set out to prove that, 'It won't happen to me!' and be at risk of proving themselves wrong from the very start.

13 Organising a training day

Introduction

People who are likely to come across problem drinkers in their day to day work are becoming increasingly interested in learning about alcoholism and problem drinking, and industry and commerce will need more and more Alcohol Education and training as the number of firms operating an Employment Alcohol Policy rises. These demands for training and education are already beginning to put a strain on specialist alcohol agencies. In some areas, demand is so great that it cannot possibly be met.

Two things need to happen. The first is that Alcohol Education should be included in all professional training courses for students who will come across problem drinkers in their future work. (This means probation officers, policemen, clergymen and teachers, for example, as well as those studying health-related subjects and social work.) The second need is for a rise in the amount of 'do-it-yourself' Alcohol Education. There is no reason why any individual or organisation should not devise a training programme on alcohol related subjects. Both local and national specialist alcohol agencies can act as resource centres to which people can turn when they need help in organising a suitable training programme.

This chapter concentrates on the 'do-it-yourself' aspect of Alcohol Education and, in particular, on organising a training day, either for colleagues, for a voluntary group you belong to or for people whose help you are counting on to set up an Alcohol Advice Centre in your area.

One day seminars

Setting up a seminar or training day involves much more than hiring a room, booking a few speakers and putting up one or two posters. A badly organised event will be poorly attended, will do very little to help those people who do turn up and will demoralise both the organisers and the speakers who have taken part.

If the day is to be a success, it needs to be well organised right from the start.

- **What do you want to achieve?**

  The idea of having a training day is often put forward in a wild burst of enthusiasm by someone who has just completed a training course himself or by someone who is interested in doing something practical to help problem drinkers. On the other hand, the idea may come from the personnel manager or the occupational health staff of a firm who are responsible for administering a new Employment Alcohol Policy.

  However it comes about, as soon as the idea of a training day has been put forward and accepted, two or three people should be made responsible for organising the event. Before any real planning is done, they need to ask themselves a few basic questions.

What will people who attend the day want to know?

Why do they need to know it?

What do they know already?

How will a training day improve their work?

Who can offer expert help to organise the day?

The answers to the first four questions should give the organisers some fairly clear aims and objectives for the day. While working on the questions, it is always a good idea to find out the views of potential members of the audience. Some people may already know something about Alcohol Education and offer their help.

The topics to be included in any training day will depend very much up on the audience. Most probation officers will already know something about the single homeless 'alcoholic' and about drunkenness offences, and health visitors will already be aware of the effects alcohol has on the body. It can be quite difficult to work out exactly what to include and what to leave out but nearly all groups are interested in discovering how to identify problem drinkers and where to refer them for help. If the group you are planning the training day for offers a counselling service, it may be useful to include a section on how to assess someone's drinking problem and so add specialised knowledge to existing skills.

After you have decided on the aims and objectives of the day, it is a good idea to contact the staff of the local Council on Alcoholism, or Alcohol Treatment Unit who will usually be glad to help you plan the day in detail and to help you find appropriate speakers. The Alcohol Education Centre (see page 224) can also help you to plan courses and can provide a consultancy service.

- ***Topics for the training day***
Courses are often planned around speakers who happen to be available but it is much better to decide exactly what topics need to be covered before booking the speakers.

Bearing the type of audience in mind, a fairly basic alcohol education training day should try to include some of the following topics.

Background information

Alcohol	Production methods
	What it is
	How it is broken down by the body
	Drink equivalents
	Availability
The extent of alcohol problems	How many people have a drink problem?
	How do we know?
	Hospital admissions for alcoholism
	Drunkenness offences
	Drinking and driving offences
	Deaths from cirrhosis of the liver
	The amount of alcohol we drink
Alcohol dependence	What is alcohol dependence?

Harm (Identifying the problem drinker)

Health	Physical
	Psychiatric
Social	Family problems
	Community problems
	Crime
	Work
	Single homeless

Treatment

Facilities	Advice centres
	Treatment units
	Accommodation

A more advanced study day might include more specialised topics connected with treatment such as:

Psychological defence mechanisms

Motivating patients

Behaviour therapy techniques

Controlled drinking

Group work (general)

Special interest groups	Women Young people Elderly
Special method groups	Social skills Psychotherapy

Counselling (general)

Counselling by telephone

- *An interesting programme?*

Checklist

Use imaginative titles

Name the speakers and say where they come from

Avoid long blocks of lecturing

Vary presentation style – workshop groups

                – case discussions

Circulate programme in advance in booklet form

Circulate fact sheet and reading list

Consider films or video

Training days are often presented in the same way time after time. What is needed is an interesting, imaginative approach to make the event more appealing, and time spent on planning and designing the programme is time well spent. A 'bad' example, but one which often appears, might look like this:

Training Day on Alcoholism

9.15	Definition of alcoholism
10.00	Medical aspects of alcoholism
11.00	*Coffee*
11.15	Alcohol problems in the family
12.00	Homeless 'alcoholics'
12.30	Discussion
12.45	*Lunch*
1.45	Methods of counselling 'alcoholics'
2.30	Alcoholics Anonymous
3.30	Discussion
4.15	*Close*

This is dull and uninteresting. The speakers' names are not given and most people will think twice about travelling any distance to turn up on the day. The morning session is very long and demands a lot of concentration. If there are more than 20 participants, people will feel inhibited when it comes to the time for discussion and will not want to speak in such a large group. One way round this problem is to split into a number of groups to join in case presentations led by the visiting speakers as in 'On the Embankment' in the revised programme on page 217.

Reorganising the programme, the first change is to give the speakers' names and to say where they come from. The next change is to devise imaginative titles which include a short description of what the session is all about. An attractively presented fact sheet and reading list, circulated before the day, will give everybody an opportunity to do some preparatory work and to be aware of some basic facts about alcohol.

In the afternoon, there could be an opportunity to split into workshop groups and four of the day's speakers could each lead a group which is particularly interested in their subject.

A reshaped programme might look like this:

The impact of drinking
A Training Day on Alcoholism

9.15	'How many people drink too much?' George Smith, Director of the Fordtown Council on Alcoholism, illustrates the size and nature of alcohol problems.

10.00   'What does the doctor say?'
        Ben Jones, Consultant Physician at Fordtown
        Infirmary, talks about common medical problems
        associated with drinking.

11.00   *Coffee*

11.15   Two forty minute case discussions on:
        'Trouble in the Family'
        Kathy Millar, Social Worker at Fordtown Social
        Services, presents a case and outlines some of the
        aspects of problem drinking in the family;
        and
        'On the Embankment'
        Geoff Masters, Coordinator of St Mary's Single
        Homeless Project, and Phil Ross, Project Social
        Worker, present cases of habitual drunken offenders
        and look at ways of helping skid row 'alcoholics'.

12.45   *Lunch*

1.45   'Talking out of drinking'
        Maggie Johnson, Counsellor at the Family Service
        Unit, outlines the methods of assessing and
        counselling problem drinkers.

2.30   'We were powerless over alcohol'
        Bill and Mary from Alcoholics Anonymous talk
        about the way that AA and Al-Anon helped them to
        rebuild their lives.

3.00   *Tea*

3.10   Group discussions
        Four small discussion groups led by visiting
        speakers which deal with questions arising from
        their own contributions and from other items in the
        programme.

4.30   *Close*

The reshaped programme breaks up the day and provides a balance between informal and formal presentation. It also makes much better use of the time available. If the programme is set out in a four sided booklet, this improves the layout and makes it look a more interesting and attractive event. If it is not possible to arrange for small groups because of limited accommodation, a useful large group exercise is a debate. This is often most useful in highlighting controversial areas such as 'Abstinence or controlled drinking?'.

Other ways of varying the programme are to arrange for a film to be shown with a specialist to answer questions afterwards or to encourage speakers to use slides to illustrate what they are saying.

Everybody who is coming to the training day should be sent a programme well in advance together with the fact sheet and reading list, and directions on how to get to the venue. It is always best if these can be put together in a folder with two or three sheets of blank paper which can be used for making notes.

Another useful idea is to arrange to have a side table where leaflets and posters are available. The local Council on Alcoholism or your local Health Education Office should be able to supply these and also tell you how to set about organising a book stall.

You need to find a comfortable, well ventilated room to hold the training day in and to make sure that it has the facilities you need. You also need to make sure that (audio) visual equipment (flipcharts, blackboards, screens, projectors and so on) will be available and working on the day.

- **Booking speakers**

Checklist

Information to give	*Information to ask for*
Subject	Fees and expenses?
Length of presentation	Type of presentation?
Details of audience	(Audio) visual equipment required?

Details of other speakers	Any special diet? (for refreshments)
Directions to the venue	A telephone number to contact?
A telephone number to contact	

You need to book speakers about three months in advance because many will be quite busy. The local Council on Alcoholism will probably be able to put you in touch with 'experts' who will be able to discuss the topics you have chosen for your training day. It is important to tell your speakers exactly what you want them to speak on and if you send them a draft programme, they will be able to tailor their presentation to fit in with the rest of the training day. Encouraging each speaker to use a different style will help to keep the audience's attention. You should always confirm the arrangements in writing and you can use the checklist in this section to make sure you have included all the relevant information.

● *Advance preparation*

Two/three months before the training day

Checklist

View and book rooms for the training day

Book (audio) visual aids

Send out invitations with closing date for applications clearly marked

Prepare programme, map and directions to the venue

Arrange for a stand-by speaker

Arrange for refreshments to be provided

Arrange for someone to act as 'rover' (see page 223).

Appoint chairperson

Preparation should start well in advance and the minimum to allow is two months. At this stage, the programme should have been planned and the speakers booked. The next important step is to find and book some suitable rooms. If you do not have all the (audio) visual aids you need, such as overhead projectors and flipcharts, you should arrange either to hire or to borrow them. It is important to check that plugs on the equipment and sockets in the rooms match!

Try and have a stand-by speaker who can fill in for anyone who fails to turn up for whatever reason. This is the time to make sure that everybody who might be interested in coming to the training day receives an invitation. When preparing the programme, fact sheet and reading list it is also useful to draw a map and give accurate directions.

Arrangements for refreshments and meals should be made and it is always worth checking with visiting speakers to find out if they have any special diet. It is useful to arrange to have someone who will act as a 'rover' and be available to attend to little problems on the day. (See 'Rover' checklist on page 223). Appoint someone to act as chairperson for the day who can introduce speakers, summarise the day as it goes along and make announcements. This may sometimes be done by one of the organisers but it is often better to have someone else so that the organisers are left free.

Ten days before the training day

Checklist

Confirm speakers by 'phone

Send out programmes, fact sheet, reading list, map and directions

Check that accommodation is not double booked

Check that (audio) visual equipment is still available

Prepare name badges, list of names and questionnaire

Give caterers provisional numbers

Confirm chairperson

Make sure 'rover' will be there

It is well worth checking everything 10 days before the event to make sure that there is no last minute panic. At this stage, the programmes should be distributed and provisional numbers given to caterers. If people attending the training day are not likely to know one another, you should make sure that name badges are prepared. It is also useful if you can have a list of everyone's name, address and occupation printed. A simple questionnaire on the seminar can be given out to everyone with the badges and it should be returned filled in at the end of the day. This may give you some ideas for improvement if you run another seminar.

Questionnaire Checklist

Did the training day change your views on alcoholism?

Did you find out any new information?

Did you like the way the day was presented?

Which sessions were most (and least) useful, and why?

What did you not understand?

What did you feel was irrelevant?

At the end of the day, did you feel more confident about identifying problem drinkers?

The day before

Check accommodation

Arrange seating plan

Fetch (audio) visual aids

Make sure plugs, cables, etc are available and working

Ring through to caterers with final numbers

Finalise arrangements with chairperson and 'rover'

Arrange to meet them half an hour before the start

Everything should be ready and prepared at this stage. The
(audio) visual aids should be collected, installed and checked
in the room where they will be used. They should be set out
at this stage but security may not allow this.

* **On the day**

Checklist

Arrive one hour before scheduled start

Check (audio) visual aids

Check seating

Check over the day with chairperson and 'rover'

Have spare programmes

Have supply of pencils

Serve refreshments away from meeting areas

Give out badges, lists of names and questionnaires

A smooth operation is the ideal but things always seem to go wrong. You should aim to arrive early so that you can check equipment and seating. A supply of spare programmes and pencils is useful and these can be given out with badges. It is better to serve tea and coffee away from the meeting area to avoid disruption.

'Rover' Checklist

Welcome speakers

Give out badges, lists of names and questionnaires

Attend to latecomers

Take messages

Pay expenses

Deal with caterers

Deal with caretaker

It is a good idea to have a 'rover' – someone with no specific responsibility – to attend to little problems such as latecomers, urgent messages, catering hitches and so on. This person can also be available to meet speakers who are arriving for the afternoon sessions, to deal with their needs and to take a note of their expenses.

● *After the day*

Checklist

Return (audio) visual aids

Write to thank speakers, chairperson, 'rover', caterers and caretaker

Assess questionnaires

Write a report

It is easy to forget everything after the day has ended but it is not a good idea to leave the (audio) visual aids where they can be stolen. Letters of thanks are always appreciated and it will be much easier to organise another training day if you have people's goodwill on your side. The replies to your questionnaires will let you know how the seminar might be modified in the light of experience and it is always useful to write your own short report so that you can keep a permanent record of how the day went.

National resources and training

There are a number of national organisations which may be able to help you to organise a successful alcohol training day. They can also advise you of the many conferences and training courses on alcohol related subjects which take place all over the country. Their addresses and telephone numbers can be found in Appendix 1.

- *Alcohol Education Centre (AEC)*
  The AEC offers the following services:

Curriculum Consultancy Service
If you want to run an event yourself but need help in deciding what to include, the AEC offers a consultancy service to advise you on education and training, goals and methods, curriculum content and structure.

Resources
A list of AEC resources for sale or hire is available on request. New resources specifically geared to education and training needs can be produced by the AEC.

Course organisation
In addition to curriculum consultancy, the AEC can administer a training programme for you. This often includes the production of all the printed material such as badges, programmes and registration packs. The AEC will also help to find appropriate speakers, to deal with the financial side of the programme, to set up a book stall and to provide a chairperson for all your sessions.

Summer schools

A basic summer school is available every year for primary health and social care agents, voluntary workers and others who come into contact with problem drinkers. The summer school provides a basic grounding in current practices and issues. An advanced summer school is available to anyone who has been on the basic summer school. The advanced summer school provides an opportunity for more advanced education on specialisations such as counselling, assessment interviews and so on.

- *National Council on Alcoholism (NCA)*
  The National Council on Alcoholism has developed a network of local Councils on Alcoholism in nearly all major centres in England and Wales. In addition to promoting conferences and study days, the NCA can put people in contact with the nearest local council, which may often be able to help in organising a local educational event. The NCA also maintains an excellent library jointly with FARE and the MCA.

- *Federation of Alcoholic Rehabilitation Establishments (FARE)*
  FARE is the national coordinating body of rehabilitation and residential establishments for problem drinkers. They specialise in the single homeless field and FARE promotes, and liaises in the planning of, specialist courses, conferences and symposia.

- *Medical Council on Alcoholism (MCA)*
  MCA promotes awareness and education within the medical profession. There are special conferences and postgraduate seminars arranged for doctors and medical students. The MCA also publishes a Journal of Alcoholism every quarter which is available on subscription.

If you live in Scotland or Northern Ireland, you should contact the appropriate national Council on Alcoholism.

14 Awkward situations

Introduction

'Alcoholics' have a reputation for getting into all sorts of sticky situations, especially after they have been drinking. When they feel they need help with these crises, at any time of the day or night, they invariably try to get in touch with whoever is trying to help them or with someone they have been told might be useful in a time of need. In fact, many agencies encourage this sort of contact but, when they do, they need to be prepared for all the problems that might follow. 'Alcoholics' also have a habit of trying to put the person who is helping them on the spot. It is a kind of game.

This chapter will be looking at some of the things that just might happen when you are working with 'alcoholics', from an incovenient telephone call to a real emergency. It also looks at some of the possible ways of dealing with them.

Telephone calls

Many agencies encourage problem drinkers or their relatives to telephone them if there is a crisis of any sort. Other agencies such as the Samaritans and Advice Centres are in the 'front line' and receive calls from people they know nothing about. Before you allow a conversation to develop, it is best to be sure that the caller knows your name and that he has given you his number if he is in a public call box. Let him talk freely for a time while you try to sense what the real problem is. Background noises such as shouting, public address systems or juke boxes may give you a clue about what is happening at the other end. If you can sound interested and willing to listen this will probably give the caller the confidence to open up. However, once you realise what the call is all about you will probably need to interrupt to get some more information. You need to know if anybody advised him to call such as his doctor or a friend, or whether he did it without someone prompting him. Other things you should find out are the caller's name, where he is calling from and whether he has called anyone else, such as the police or social services. Most important of all, you should make sure you understand exactly what the problem is.

Checklist

Give the caller your name

Get the caller's telephone number

Let the caller talk freely

Listen for background noises

Did anyone tell the caller to telephone?

What is the caller's name?

Has he called anyone else?

What is the problem?

Write it all down

Although each call for help is different from any other and needs to be handled with this in mind, some types of call fall into categories for which it is possible to offer guidelines.

- **Calls from someone you know nothing about**

  'I've got a friend with a drinking problem'
  This type of call is often made by someone who is genuinely concerned about a friend and it can be dealt with by offering advice about what facilities are available for help, or by offering to send a pamphlet. However, it is not unknown for the 'friend' to be the person who is calling. This is one way for a caller to find out what help is available without saying who he is. Sometimes, he will come clean after a few minutes by saying, 'Actually it's not my friend, it's me'. The friend has been invented because there are no friends the caller can turn to and it is important to encourage him either to call again or to make a definite appointment to come in and see you.

Advise caller of facilities available

Send pamphlet

Is it the caller who has the problem?

If so, offer appointment

- ### *Calls from people you may or may not know*

'My husband's drinking again'
This problem often arises when a husband has been pressurised into treatment by his wife threatening to leave.

If the wife has been involved in her husband's treatment, she may well have some idea that it was always possible for him to go back to drinking and she may just want to be reassured that she can cope. However, she may also need help in facing up to the problem of dealing with the distress of a husband who is drinking again and who may be abusive and aggressive. If there is any risk of physical violence you may need to involve the police. Any demands for a visit to the home to stop her husband drinking should be resisted because they are not likely to succeed.

By telephoning, the wife has been able to share her problem but she still needs support. An offer to see them both in a day or two will give her something to look forward to and to talk over with her husband when he sobers up. It is rare for the husband to be so drunk that his life is at risk but this should always be checked.

Checklist

Allow her to share her problem

Remember that it is she who now has the problem

Is there any physical violence?

Do not agree to visit the home

Offer an appointment

How drunk is the husband?

'I am about to take an overdose'
This is the classical 'cry for help' and callers of this type are trying to get your full attention. The likelihood of the caller taking an overdose may well be low (though not always, of course) and it could be that all he wants is support. Talk to the caller for as long as practically possible and try to identify possible reasons why he feels distressed.

If he says that he can see no way out of some problem and that he cannot face up to things, it is probably best to try and encourage him to see a positive side to the situation. It is difficult to find anything humorous in a call like this but if the caller can see the lighter side it is a good sign. Try to give him some hope by offering a telephone number he can ring outside your office hours and make him feel welcome to pop in and talk things over in person. If the call is made from a private telephone, you can call back later to check on what has happened. If you know the caller, you should know whether a visit to his home (or wherever he is at the time) is advisable.

Checklist

Hold caller as long as possible

Try to find the positive side

Look for a lighter side

Offer an alternative number

Offer to see the caller

Ring back later

'I've taken an overdose'
This is one of the most difficult cases to deal with. 'Alcoholics' are 50 times more prone to suicide than the general population

and so you need to take a call like this seriously. You need to find out what drugs the caller has taken, how much, when and with how much alcohol. If he gives clear answers to your questions, he will probably be able to seek medical help by ringing his GP or by going to the Accident and Emergency Department at the local hospital.

On the other hand, if his speech is slurred and he does not seem to respond to your questions, you will need to alert the ambulance and police services *immediately*, on another line if possible, so that you can keep the caller talking. If in doubt, err on the side of safety.

Checklist

What drugs or tablets?

How many?

How much drink?

If responsive – advise him to ring GP or to go to Accident and Emergency Department

If unresponsive – alert emergency services

Ringing you at home late at night
One of the difficulties about 'alcoholics' is that they refuse to confine their problems to office hours. Crises often develop late at night and if a problem drinker has developed a close and trusting relationship with you, it can be very easy to think 'Oh, he won't mind me ringing him at home just this once'. This often happens when the 'alcoholic' has been drinking and has little control over an impulse to ring you. It is important to try not to be annoyed, even when you have got out of the bath to answer the telephone. Be quite firm and explain that there is little that can be done to help late at night. Explain that you are prepared to see the caller the next day, or after the weekend. When he next turns up at the office, you must always try to avoid being purposely brusque or rude. If you give your number to a problem drinker, you can almost expect him to ring. In some cases, he might also give the number to his friends. The only way to try to make

sure you do not get calls at inconvenient times is to avoid giving your number in the first place.

Try not to be annoyed

Be firm

Arrange to see the problem drinker in office hours

Avoid giving your telephone number in the first place

Coping with aggression

People who have been drinking are often aggressive. Problem drinkers often seem to blame the person who is trying to help them when things go wrong and they can become verbally abusive and sometimes physically violent. If an 'alcoholic' called in to the office and calmly announced, 'I'm feeling quite annoyed', it would not have quite the same impact as, 'If you don't get me some help I'll smash this place up!'

It always seems to happen that the aggressive 'alcoholics' are the ones who arrive at the most inconvenient moments and it is easy to react in a way which might be interpreted as unhelpful. This usually makes them more aggressive. If you think carefully before you speak, it might avoid a punch-up in the office! If the problem drinker is determined to make his feelings known with force, the first thing you should do is to make sure that other people are safely out of the firing range and that they do not give him an audience to play to. This also means that he will not lose face if he does not carry out his threats. Physical contact must be avoided if at all possible and you should try to ensure that an escape route is available. Try to distract the aggression by changing the subject.

Checklist

Do not respond with aggression

Ensure the safety of other people

Maintain an escape route

Remove the possible audience

Avoid physical contact

Try to distract the aggression by changing the subject

Respecting anonymity

- ### *Refusing to give a name and address*
  A problem drinker may refuse to give his name and address
  because he does not want anyone to know about his problem.
  It is possible that he is ashamed of himself or that he may lose
  his job if his drink problem is discovered. People sometimes
  travel great distances to be certain of anonymity. Your priority
  should not be to find out his name and address at all costs
  but to maintain contact and to offer him a feeling of security.
  However, you must make it clear that you expect him to be
  open and honest with you after a few sessions. You also need
  to tell him exactly where you stand with regard to confidentiality. It would be wrong to allow a train driver or an airline
  pilot to continue working if he was drinking heavily. In a case
  like this, it would only be possible to promise confidentiality
  if he agreed to stop work until he had been treated
  successfully.

Checklist

Maintain contact

Emphasise the need for honesty

State your own position on confidentiality

- ### *Refusing to allow you to contact other agencies*
  If a problem drinker refuses to allow you to contact other
  agencies, it may simply reflect his fear of other people knowing about his drinking. The fear may be very understandable
  if, for example, it meant that his children would be put into

care. On the other hand, it may be a more selfish fear. If a problem drinker's own doctor knew about his drinking, he may stop prescribing tranquillisers. Once more, it is important to make your own position on confidentiality quite clear. Different disciplines have different ethical and legal obligations; a social worker who suspects child abuse must investigate and a hospital doctor who finds out about a drink problem is ethically compelled to inform the patient's general practitioner.

Checklist

State your own position on confidentiality

Be sure of ethical and legal obligations

Dealing with drunk 'alcoholics'

● ***Appointment with an 'alcoholic' who is intoxicated***
It is not unusual for 'alcoholics' to arrive for appointments the worse for wear. It is even more likely for them to be drunk when visited at home. For the most part, any attempt to have a constructive conversation will be a waste of time. The 'alcoholic' will often not remember much of what is said, including his abusive language! The question to ask yourself is, 'Has he got drunk because he was going to see me or would he have got drunk anyway?' If he does appear to have got drunk because he was going to see you, he may have been trying to tell you something, perhaps how bad his problem was and you should make it clear that you have understood.

Whatever his reason may be for getting drunk, you should make it clear that you disapprove of his drinking but at the same time make it clear that you are not rejecting him as a person. The only thing you can sensibly do is to make another appointment in writing.

Checklist

Do not waste time with an interview

Be vigorously disapproving of the 'alcoholic's' drinking

Do not reject him as a person

Make another written appointment

- ### Intoxicated 'alcoholics' with tablets
  It is not unusual to be faced with an 'alcoholic' who is both drunk and in possession of tablets. You may discover this by accident or the 'alcoholic' may threaten to take an overdose if his demands for money or accommodation are not met. In either case, you should be concerned about the possibility of an overdose or about the effect that some drugs have when taken with alcohol. It may seem that the easiest thing to do is simply to take the tablets away but this raises ethical, moral and legal dilemmas. The tablets may have been prescribed or may have been acquired illegally but they are the 'alcoholic's' property and to take them away is technically theft.

  You should make it quite clear that it is entirely the 'alcoholic's' own decision to take an overdose and that no-one else can be held responsible. You can then go on to point out the advantages of going about things in a different way and end up by offering to help him.

  You should try to find out what the tablets are and why they are being taken. If they are for a condition such as heart failure or diabetes it may be dangerous to take them away. On the other hand, if they are tranquillisers or antidepressants you should try to contact the person who prescribed them to see if they are really necessary in view of the risk of an overdose and the effect which they have when taken with alcohol. Tablets which have been acquired illegally should be given to the police, with the problem drinker's consent.

Checklist

Risk of an overdose?

Risk of effects of the tablets and alcohol together?

Place the responsibility of an overdose with the 'alcoholic'

Find out the reason for taking drugs

Discuss the case with the person who prescribed the tablets if possible

Missed appointments

- **Failing to turn up at your office**
One of the frustrations of working with 'alcoholics' is that they tend not to come and see you when things seem to be going well to their way of thinking. This usually means there is not a crisis, not that great progress is being made towards recovery. Vigorous follow up after treatment often helps to increase the chances of success and it is important to find out why an appointment has been missed. A telephone call or a letter may be best to begin with and, if this fails, the next step is a personal visit. You may well be told what you can do with your help and it is best to be prepared for this. All you can do is to press on regardless with offers of further follow up. You should only stop seeing someone after careful consideration.

Checklist

Vigorous follow up helps to increase the chances of success

Make personal contact whenever possible

Only stop follow up after serious consideration

- **No reply at the house**
Arranging to visit someone at home and then finding there is no reply when you arrive is infuriating at the best of times. However, if it is quite out of character for the person to miss appointments, or if you feel there may be someone in the house because a light is on or noises can be heard, you may have reason to be suspicious. It could be that someone is in but is too intoxicated to answer the door, is suffering severe withdrawal symptoms or is unconscious from an overdose of tablets. He may even have had a heart attack or be suffering from some other medical condition.
Whatever you do will be wrong! If you break the door down,

the person will have popped out to the shops. If you leave an appointment card, he will be found dead from an overdose! What you do must depend on circumstances but it is always worth asking neighbours if they have seen the person recently or if they have a key to get in. If the neighbours cannot help and you still feel you should get in, the police should be able to help.

Checklist

If circumstances are *not* suspicious, leave your visiting card

If the circumstances *are* suspicious, try to get in by asking for help from neighbours or calling the police to perhaps force an entry

---

Finding someone unconscious

If you find an 'alcoholic' who appears to be dead or unconscious, the first thing to do is to look for signs of life. Movements of the chest will indicate that he is breathing. You could also feel for a pulse in the neck (feel just in front of the angle of the jaw). If he is unconscious you should lay him flat and on his left side, making sure that he can breathe easily (it may help to pull up the chin and to check to see that the mouth is not obstructed by vomit or false teeth). If there is any obvious injury you should stop the bleeding by applying pressure to the wound. Now is the time to find help if it has not been possible before and someone should call for an ambulance. After this, do not leave the unconscious person until the ambulance arrives. You should note any tablets or empty bottles which may be lying around and look for any recently written notes or letters. If you suspect that the person is dead, you should call for both police and ambulance and treat him as if he were unconscious.

Checklist

Lay the person flat on his left side

Make sure he can breathe freely

Apply pressure to any bleeding points

Call an ambulance

Look for tablets and empty bottles

Look for notes

Helping out

• ***Nowhere to sleep***
If a request for shelter and for money to pay for it is made before two o'clock, there is a fair chance you will be able to help. You should offer a list of places where accommodation can be found and write a letter to the manager of the local DHSS office, explaining the circumstances and asking for discretionary help. However, requests for help like this are normally made when it is impossible to do anything, although there are Government Resettlement Units and night shelters in some of the larger cities which accept referrals and make no charge for accommodation. It is important to remember that it is up to the problem drinker to find his own bed and money, no matter how much he tries to make you feel guilty and personally responsible.

Checklist

Give the problem drinker a list of likely accommodation

Provide him with a letter to DHSS

Tell him about night shelters

Do not feel guilty!

• ***On the scrounge***
Problem drinkers, especially skid row 'alcoholics', never seem to have any trouble in thinking of good reasons for asking for money to buy more drink. If they beg the price of a cup of tea

three times, they can then buy a bottle of cider. Other requests for finance include asking for the money to buy a packet of razor blades (advise them to grow a beard), for the money to get to Nottingham where they have a job waiting (give them directions to the motorway and advise them to use a thumb) and for the money to buy a packet of cigarettes (offer a lecture on bronchitis). It is never helpful to provide actual cash if only because the word will go round that you are a 'good touch'. In fact, some agencies do budget for cash to be used in this way but it is best to use vouchers or warrants whenever possible. If you are asked for money for a sandwich, you can always offer to go the nearest snack bar to buy it. They often decide that they do not feel hungry after all!

Checklist

Avoid giving out cash

Issue vouchers or warrants whenever possible

Offer to buy what the 'alcoholic' has asked for rather than give him money

Meeting 'alcoholics' in pubs

After you have worked in an area for a while, you are almost bound to meet some of the people you have helped when you are enjoying a quiet drink in a local pub. Such a meeting may be quite pleasant, but often it is not. One difficulty is that 'alcoholics' often want to buy you drinks. You should always refuse politely. If the barman gives you a drink that has already been paid for, you should accept it with thanks but you should not buy one back. In short, whenever you meet people you have helped, you are in effect at work and so it would be irresponsible to buy drinks for people who are physically damaged by alcohol or who are aiming to be abstinent. You may well decide to move on to another pub fairly soon! It can be a problem when the drinker becomes abusive or makes fun of you. In a situation such as this you can leave, ignore what is going on or make disapproving comments; you should not get involved in any argument or slanging match.

Checklist

Be friendly and do not make any comment on the problem drinker being in the pub

Refuse any drinks offered by him

Do not buy him any drinks

Model sensible drinking

Go somewhere else if it gets too much

'I want to help the others'

After two or three weeks without drinking, 'alcoholics' have often felt such great benefits themselves that they want to share them with other people. The reason for this may be their strong identification with you as a person who has been of great help to them and in some way they want to be like you. There is no reason why some successfully recovered problem drinkers should not help and in many areas counselling facilities for problem drinkers are largely staffed by ex–'alcoholics'. Alcoholics Anonymous, of course, is based on the principle of helping fellow sufferers. However, there are certain aspects to bear in mind:

Checklist

The problem drinker must have been abstinent or improved for at least six months

Education and training will be required

A high level of support will be needed

Postscript: how do you tell him?

How do you tell someone that you think he has a drink problem? Some alcohol specialists say that it is like a doctor trying to tell a patient that he has cancer; rarely easy. However, there are ways in which you can prepare yourself.

You need to convince yourself that, in all probability, the problem will not just go away if it is ignored. It will only get worse. Once a problem drinker has been identified, he needs to be made aware of his problem as soon as possible. He has to accept the idea that he has a drink problem before any advice or treatment you offer can be permanently effective.

Once you feel that it is right to talk to someone about his drink problem, it helps to be prepared for your own reactions to what might happen. The problem drinker's replies may well make you feel embarrassed and ashamed for ever having brought the subject up. Typical replies might be, 'You don't really believe I've got a drink problem, do you?' or, 'No, you're joking, me? A drink problem?' Besides trying to make you feel embarrassed and ashamed, the problem drinker may also play upon your fear of being rejected by him and you should be prepared to be told what you can do with your offer of help! Fortunately, this rejection is often short-lived.

You should also expect the problem drinker to deny that his drinking is causing him any problems although, like a cancer patient, he may often suspect that something is wrong. He does not want to believe what he is told. This may mean that he becomes angry and aggressive towards you. If you are prepared for these reactions, it means that you will not be led into any arguments which may completely break any relationship you have built up.

The first time you bring problem drinking into the conversation, you should be aiming to sow the seed of an idea in the drinker's mind. When you return to the subject in a later conversation, he may have thought about what you said and agree that it might help to talk to you or someone else who has helped other people in a situation similar to his own.

The question of exactly how to bring problem drinking into the conversation is a tricky one. Unless someone needs urgent medical attention, it is probably not a good idea to be too direct. You should avoid talking about 'alcoholics' and alcoholism because both these terms can be highly emotionally charged. A useful approach is to begin by talking about drinking in general, about alcohol as a drug and about the harm it can cause. You can then lead on to more specific questions about the effects which drink is having on the drinker's life. It is probably best to start by talking about the areas of his life which seem to be least affected by drink. For example, if someone was having real problems with his family because of drinking, you should begin by asking about the effect it has on his work. In this way, you will not immediately threaten the problem drinker and he will probably be more willing to go on to discuss the more serious aspects of the problem and to think about your offer of help. In some cases, it may be helpful to talk about the reasons you have for suspecting a drink problem. However, it is important to remember that each problem drinker is an individual and will react in his own way. The only guide to the 'right time' to bring up the subject of problem drinking is your own intuition.

These guidelines, like the rest of this book, are based on the authors' own experience. They have been tried and they have worked but this does not mean to say that they will work in every case. They should be taken and tested, and then modified in the light of personal experience.

Anyone can offer help to a problem drinker but you need to remember that it is all too easy to get out of your depth. There are specialist alcohol agencies in most parts of Great Britain which can offer their help and support to both the problem drinker and to the person who is helping him. You should make full use of them.

Appendix 1: useful addresses

Al-anon
Family Groups (UK and Eire)
61 Great Dover Street,
London SE1 4YF
Tel (01) 403 0888 (*Alateen* can also be contacted through this address)

Alcohol Education Centre
The Maudsley Hospital, 99 Denmark Hill, London SE5 8AZ
Tel (01) 703 8053

Alcoholics Anonymous
(General Service Office UK)
PO Box 514, 11 Redcliffe Gardens, London SW10
Tel (01) 352 9779

Fare
(Federation of Alcoholic Rehabilitation Establishments)
3 Grosvenor Crescent, London SW1X 7EE
Tel (01) 235 0609/0

Medical Council on Alcoholism
3 Grosvenor Crescent, London SW1X 7EE
Tel (01) 235 4182

National Council on Alcoholism
3 Grosvenor Crescent, London SW1X 7EE
Tel (01) 235 4182

Tacade
(Teachers' Advisory Council on Alcohol and Drug Education)
Professional training in education and counselling about all forms of drug use and abuse
2 Mount Street, Manchester M2 5NG
Tel (061) 834 7210

Scottish Council on Alcoholism
47/49 York Place, Edinburgh EH1 3JD
Tel (031) 556 0459

Northern Ireland Council on Alcohol
36/40 Victoria Street, Belfast BT1
Tel Belfast 38173

South Glamorgan Alcoholism Information & Advice Service
13 Richmond Crescent, Cardiff, Wales
Tel (0222) 499499

To find out if there is a Council on Alcoholism in your area, you should contact the appropriate national body. Your Local Authority Social Service Department or Health Authority will be able to tell you about Health Education resources and all local facilities.

The *Directory of Projects* (England and Wales) contains details of all types of accommodation and information services for people with drinking problems. It is published every two years and is available from: FARE (Federation of Alcoholic Rehabilitation Establishments), 3 Grosvenor Crescent, London SW1X 7EE. Tel (01) 235 0609/0

If you want help with your own drinking you should either see your own doctor, contact your local Council on Alcoholism (number in the telephone directory) or a local AA group (number in the telephone directory).

Appendix 2: alcohol content of some common drinks

	% absolute alcohol by volume		grams of absolute alcohol
Beer, lager, ordinary cider	4%	½ pint Can (275 ml)	9 8.5
Table wine	10%	Glass Bottle 1 litre bottle	9 60 79
Rough cider	13%	½ pint	29
Barley wine	17%	Bottle (6 oz)	38
Sherry, port, vermouth	18%	Large glass Bottle (760 ml)	12 108
Whisky, gin, rum, brandy, vodka	40%	Single ½ bottle 1 bottle (760 ml)	7.5 120 240
Methylated spirit, surgical spirit	95%	½ pint	213

Appendix 3: further reading

Alcoholism – a changing view
ARMOR, D. J. et al. *Alcoholism and treatment* Wiley, 1978.
EDWARDS, G. and GRANT, M. *Alcoholism: new knowledge and new responses* Croom Helm, 1977.
EDWARDS, G. and GRANT, M. eds. *Alcoholism treatment in transition* Croom Helm, 1980.
ROYAL COLLEGE OF PSYCHIATRISTS *Alcohol and alcoholism: report of the Special Committee* Tavistock Publications, 1979.

The problem drinker and the family
BURTON, M. *An alcoholic in the family* Faber, 1974.
CAMBERWELL COUNCIL ON ALCOHOLISM *Women and alcohol* Tavistock Publications, paperback 1980.
CORRIGAN, E. M. *Alcoholic women in treatment* OUP, 1980.
WALROND-SKINNER, S. *Family therapy: treatment of natural systems* Routledge, 1976.

Drinking and work
HORE, B. and PLANT, M. eds. *Alcohol problems in employment* Croom Helm, 1981.
PLANT, M. *Drinking careers: occupations, drinking habits and drinking problems* Tavistock Publications, 1979.

Down and out on skid row
COOK, T. *Vagrancy: some new perspectives* Academic Press, cased and paperback 1979.
OTTO, S. and ORFORD, J. *Not quite like home: small hostels for alcoholics and others* Wiley, 1978.

Alcoholics Anonymous
ROBINSON, D. *Talking out of alcoholism: the self-help process of Alcoholics Anonymous* Croom Helm, cased and paperback 1979.

The group approach
PRIESTLEY, P. et al. *Social skills and personal problem solving: a handbook of methods* Tavistock Publications, cased and paperback 1978.

DOUGLAS, T. *Basic group-work* Tavistock Publications, 1978.
DOUGLAS, T. *Group-work practice* Tavistock Publications, 1976.

Working with young people

GRANT, M. ed. *Alcohol education for young people in Scotland* Alcohol Education Centre, 1980.
HAWKER, A. *Adolescents and alcohol* B. Edsall, 1978.
O'CONNOR, J. *The young drinkers: a cross-national study of social and cultural influences* Tavistock Publications, 1978.

General

MADDEN, J. S. et al. *Aspects of alcohol and drug dependence* Pitman Medical, 1980.
OFFICE OF POPULATION CENSUSES AND SURVEYS Social Survey Division *Drinking in England and Wales: an enquiry carried out on behalf of the DHSS* by P. Wilson. HMSO, 1980.
HOME OFFICE Research Unit *Alcoholism and social policy: are we on the right lines?* by M. Tuck. HMSO, 1980.

Appendix 4: alcohol and the law in England and Wales

Young people and the law

Persons under 18 years	may not be supplied with intoxicants in bars or off-licences; may not drink intoxicants in bars or off-licences; may not buy intoxicants from bars or off-licences; may not be employed in bars or licensed premises;
Persons between 16 and 18	may be supplied with beer, porter, cider or perry on licensed premises with a meal, provided the meal is not served in a bar.
Persons between 14 and 16	may be in a bar of licensed premises during permitted hours but may not buy, be supplied with or consume intoxicants. They may be legally *supplied with* intoxicants in clubs.
Children under 14 years	may not be in the bar of licensed premises during permitted hours but may legally *be present* in clubs and may *consume* intoxicants there.
Children under 5 years	may not be given intoxicants except on medical orders.

Note: Although the Licensing Act 1964 allows young people under 18 to drink alcoholic drinks in clubs, a licensing authority has the power to make restrictions. Club rules may also impose their own restrictions.

Adults and the law – some relevant points which are not widely known

The Licensing Act 1964 places certain restrictions on licensees. It is illegal for a publican or his staff to serve intoxicants to someone who is obviously drunk.

It is also illegal for any person to procure intoxicants for an obviously drunken person.

Drinking and Driving and the law

Under the Road Safety Act of 1967, it is an offence to drive with blood alcohol level of more than 80 mg%.

Acknowledgements

Ian Davies and Duncan Raistrick would like to thank ROBIN DAVIDSON, Senior Psychologist, Addiction Unit, Leeds, for his special contribution of original research to Chapters 1 and 9, JOHN WYMARK-HOAR, Coordinator, Leeds Detoxification Centre, for work on the single homeless in Chapter 6, and DR P. M. J. O'BRIEN, Consultant Psychiatrist, Scalebor Park, for the account of the Alcohol Treatment Unit in Chapter 8 and his ideas on outcome in Chapter 11.

The authors would also like to thank Salli Hornsby for her patience in producing the typed manuscripts.

Index